Praise for John Lee:

"John Lee is known for his immediately practical
and refreshing approach to problems that we all
face at work and at home."

—KAREN C. BLICHER, LCSW, CHT,
Director of Mental Health Education,
Mountain Area Health Education Center,
Asheville, North Carolina

"John Lee is one of the greatest teachers in the
United States."

—ROBERT BLY

The Anger Solution

Other books by John Lee:

The Flying Boy: Healing the Wounded Man

The Flying Boy II: The Journey Continues

*Facing the Fire: Experiencing and
Expressing Anger Appropriately*

*Growing Yourself Back Up:
Understanding Emotional Regression*

*The Missing Peace:
Solving the Anger Problem for
Alcoholics/Addicts and Those Who Love Them*

Recovery: Plain and Simple

THE

Anger Solution

*The Proven Method for Achieving Calm
and Developing Healthy,
Long-lasting Relationships*

John Lee

Da Capo
∞
LIFE
LONG

A MEMBER OF THE PERSEUS BOOKS GROUP

Set in 11 point Electra by the Perseus Books Group

Library of Congress Cataloging-in-Publication Data
Lee, John H., 1951-
    The anger solution : the proven method for achieving calm and developing healthy, long-lasting relationships / John Lee.
        p. cm.
    Includes bibliographical references and index.
    ISBN 978-0-7382-1260-9 (alk. paper)
    1. Anger. 2. Behavior modification. 3. Regression (Psychology) 4. Interpersonal relations. I. Title.
    BF575.A5L438 2009
    152.4'7—dc22
                        2009007837

First Da Capo Press edition 2009

Published by Da Capo Press
A Member of the Perseus Books Group
www.dacapopress.com

Da Capo Press books are available at special discounts for bulk purchases in the U.S. by corporations, institutions, and other organizations. For more information, please contact the Special Markets Department at the Perseus Books Group, 2300 Chestnut Street, Suite 200, Philadelphia, PA, 19103, or call (800) 810-4145, ext. 5000, or e-mail special.markets@perseusbooks.com.

10 9 8 7 6 5 4 3 2

For my wife,

Susan,

who is my inspiration, editor, fan, best friend,
and one of the least angry people I've ever known.

Anybody can become angry—that is easy, but to be angry with the right person and to the right degree and at the right time and for the right purpose, and in the right way—that is not easy.

—ARISTOTLE

The past isn't dead. It's not even the past.

—WILLIAM FAULKNER

CONTENTS

Introduction

Anger is a universal emotion that has touched all of us. You wouldn't have picked up this book if anger has not been pervasive in your life. I began exploring, experiencing, and explaining my feelings, ideas, and approach to the most misunderstood emotion called anger over twenty-five years ago, when I published my first national best seller, *The Flying Boy: Healing the Wounded Man.* Since then, I have spoken in over fifty cities a year all over the world and counseled and coached thousands of men, women, couples, co-workers, CEOs, counselors, and therapists.

The material here has been perfected over these many years; prior to now, it's been presented piecemeal. *The Anger Solution* pulls all this information together into a cohesive and easy read. This is the only anger book that not only sheds a positive light on this emotion, but it also gives hope to anyone who will practice these exercises and processes.

Anger is a fact of life that affects everyone, some more than others. We all have been angry or been around those who are angry, and most of us have thought that the world would be better off without this emotion. But here's the real truth: Anger is not your enemy. In fact, it can be your ally—one that can save your relationship, your job, and your peace of mind. Anger can heal relationships of all kinds, creating greater closeness and intimacy.

Once you learn how to express anger appropriately you will see that it can "clear the air," tear down walls of misunderstanding, and, most of all, not hurt anyone (including yourself). Perhaps you have had very little, if any, experience with appropriate expressions of anger. You may even believe it isn't possible. *The Anger Solution* will help you navigate this path to healing.

We all know holding it in, bottling it up, or denying this powerful emotion does not work. Neither does exploding. What does work is expressing anger appropriately. The word *appropriately* is the key because what most of us have seen is anger or rage expressed in a dysfunctional and toxic manner and not in a way that works for all involved. As those who have attended my workshops, seminars, and private sessions have found, it is not anger that causes people pain. The truth about anger is it can be healthy, positive, productive, and pivotal in helping or creating communication and cleaner conversation, and is not a "negative" emotion as many claim it is.

In addition to discussing anger, this book will delve into the topic of passivity. One of the main reasons for putting this material in an anger book is because all the writers of academic texts agree that one of the main ways to treat passivity is to treat it as an inverted form of anger.

My approach to anger works where most fail. It is unlike any other anger management program you've ever attended or heard of. This program includes a lot of things others don't, but perhaps one of the most significant benefits about my method is what it does *not* include.

The Anger Solution is free of:
Guilt

Instead of feeling guilty about your emotions or your inability to conduct yourself appropriately, you will understand that you couldn't possibly do something you were never taught. If your parents, teachers, and other authority figures didn't model expressing anger correctly, then how would you know how to do it?

Shame

You are not less than, defective, or maladjusted. With the right information and tools, you can learn how to be angry without feeling or causing pain.

Resentment

Freedom of choice takes away the resentment. Nobody is making you do this. You are empowering yourself by learning how to face your true feelings.

Embarrassment

You are not alone; far from it! Most everyone struggles with anger. But in this book, you'll see your story told many times over by other people.

Hopelessness

After you realize that your inappropriate anger has hurt those you love or work with, you may feel that you are stuck in this pattern of not being able to express or contain your emotions. But this book will show you that there's hope, understanding, and even joy when you learn how to manage your anger.

Many traditional approaches to anger offer valuable tools. However, there's one critical key that often gets neglected. Jack is an anger-management participant who "graduates" from a workshop and goes home armed with anger-blocking techniques. Jack may have learned to deal with his anger—but when he goes home or back to work, he realizes the people he interacts with every day have not taken the same course! Jack's triumphant mastery of his volatile emotions unfortunately means little when he's surrounded by people who are still experiencing anger in an unhealthy and counterproductive manner. Sadly, most people like Jack fall right back into their unwanted behaviors fairly quickly.

Employees see the boss raging, so the employee rages. We know that children's main way of learning is through modeling, so if they see a parent expressing anger inappropriately, they integrate these behaviors and actions into their own expressions of anger.

The Anger Solution does truly offer a solution: You can use it before you get angry, while you're angry, and after the anger has passed. This method is flexible, easy to learn, and easy to teach.

One of the key elements of this program is the recognition that there is such a thing as "good," healthy anger. Where most people get stuck is in distinguishing it from "bad," unhealthy anger — what we'll call rage. In this book, you'll learn what rage really is — one of the leading causes of distance, disasters, and divorces. Teenagers run away from home because of the rage, not the anger. Employees quit jobs because of raging bosses, not angry ones. Spouses leave husbands and wives due to undue, amounts of rage — not anger.

Most important, this book will also show you how to work through your unhealthy anger, via understanding and implementing what I call "the best-kept secret in psychology" — emotional regression. In *The Anger Solution*, this important psychological, emotional, physical, and spiritual phenomenon is crucial to working with anger and rage along with other powerful emotions such as fear, sadness, grief, and frustration. Once emotional regression is included in working with the angry or raging person, much more can be achieved and accomplished, and therein lies the gift of achieving healthy relationships.

I can't stress enough how regression is a critical element in anger and rage. Exploring emotional regression is a major factor in separating anger—your healthy, beneficial emotions—from rage, the emotions and actions that tear you up and tear up your family and friends, too. This book will help you clearly see how regression impacts upon daily life both at home and at work. It will also give you the tools to express anger appropriately.

With this book, I'm offering The Detour Method™ an easy-to-learn and easy-to-use six-step process that can literally save relationships, create deeper connections, and dissipate rage. It is a proven way to minimize, reduce, and even eliminate much time-consuming, energy-draining conflicts and confrontations. The Detour Method is a proven process that has helped thousands of people improve and enhance all kinds of relationships. It incorporates the differences between anger and rage, and couples this with the reality that overreactions (or in more simple terms, "making a mountain out of a molehill") are more about the past than about the present.

Finally, *The Anger Solution* is an important part of your ability to increase or enhance your EQ—emotional intelligence quotient. Emotional intelligence is the key to not only achieving successful careers but essential in achieving thriving, less stressful, and more fulfilling relationships.

I've written this book for the growing number of people who desire more rewarding relationships in all areas of their lives. Do you want deeper connection, enhanced communication, and the ability to express a full range of emotions? *The Anger Solution* can help, heal, and stop the hurting. As we know, the old childhood rhyme, "Sticks and stones may break my bones but words may never hurt me," is a flat-out lie. Words wound, words hurt, and words heal. I hope the following words bring some healing to anyone who has been wounded by inappropriate words and actions.

Chapter 1

Anger: The Real Story

We all have our definitions of anger. Anger is a feeling, an emotion that is neither positive nor negative, although most clinicians, therapists, and authors have labeled it as the latter. Anger is no more destructive than sadness or loneliness. Fear is often far more destructive than is anger.

Many currently practicing mental health professionals believe that anger is simply a cover; like out-of-control ivy in a well-manicured yard. They contend that underneath anger is the real issue that lurks and hurts people: fear. They believe if they can help patients, parents, and partners pull off this cover and deal with what frightens them, then their anger will magically disappear.

Essentially stated, the message is, "You are not angry. You are afraid," or "Your anger is merely covering up your sadness or disappointment." This point of view is couched under the heading of, "You are not feeling what you say you are feeling. Let's get to the real emotions underneath your anger."

This traditional approach defines primary emotions as sadness, loneliness, fear, joy, love, and so on. But anger, say these professionals, is a secondary emotion.

However, my experience has shown that anger is a primal feeling that anyone with a pulse experiences weekly, if not daily. It is an essential emotion: You can't and shouldn't avoid anger.

Jeremy discovered his wife of five years, Samantha, had her tubes tied without discussing it with him. This was after they had both declared that becoming parents was a life goal.

In therapy, Jeremy expressed his anger at his wife half a dozen times. After hearing this, their couple's counselor said, "Jeremy, my guess is you're not really angry so much as you are disappointed and scared that you and Samantha won't stay together without children."

When Jeremy told me this story he half-jokingly said he became so angry at the therapist that he wanted to punch him. Instead he got up and walked out, saying to his wife as he left, "I'm not going to sit here and listen to someone tell me I'm not feeling what I have every right to feel."

What Jeremy experienced is what we have all felt. Anger is energy that pulses through the human body, brain, and soul. When this energy is expelled appropriately from a person, not only does the person expressing anger feel more energized, but no one is hurt or worse for the expression. However, if this life force is suppressed, repressed, bottled up, stuffed, or swallowed, there are profound negative repercussions and consequences to both the person and those around him or her. This is why so many think of anger as being solely negative—they are seeing the damage done by anger that has been held in and not expressed appropriately.

When I ask clients or workshop participants who they are most angry at most of the time, 80 to 90 percent will declare it to be themselves. In other words, they have turned their anger inward, where it has not only failed to diminish but has increased from remaining pent up. If you stay stuck in a place for too long without expressing anger, then you'll feel sadness. Although sadness and anger are two primary emotions that go hand in hand, they are not the same feeling and cannot therefore be used interchangeably.

Anger is meant to circulate like a spring. As long as that anger is about current injustices, slights, wrongs, hurts, rejections, or slanders, and given release, it will flow up and out into the world, not down and back into your body, and will produce positive results both inside and outside you.

If employed and expressed appropriately, this powerful emotion can be used to move individuals, couples, families, corporations, and nations out of dead-end or abusive situations or relationships.

The women's movement was fueled by an anger that was overdue. The outcome forever changed the world we live for the better. Rosa Parks's anger in 1955 is what contributed to her and a whole race of people from being stuck at the back of the bus. Anger is what got our country out of Vietnam.

Can you imagine someone saying this to Gloria Steinem or Rosa Parks or the Vietnam vets, for that matter, "You're not really angry; you're just scared"?

Why Everyone Tries to Avoid Anger

We've been taught and threatened with the belief that anger is bad, negative, uncivilized, rude, and unacceptable. Add these to the misinformation and misconceptions that anger leads to more anger and that expressing anger increases blood pressure and heart problems, and it is no wonder we are racked with guilt and shame, and increasingly tamp down and numb our emotions.

Everyone from parents to teachers and pastors have been telling children things like, "Good girls and boys don't get angry," for generations. And what about, "It's not ladylike." Girls have been told they are bitches, ball busters, nags, hags, and witches if they get angry. Boys have been taught to think of "angry" women that way. We wonder why women are angry— well, just look at what they are called when they express their emotions!

Most people—of all educational backgrounds, incomes, religious persuasions, and inclinations—have it in their heads, hearts, or rear ends that anger equals pain.

When someone got angry in our childhood, we felt the slaps, hits, silent treatment, and icy stares. We were punished by being sent to bed without supper or exiled to our bedroom or boarding school. In other words, when someone got angry, someone got hurt.

Somewhere in our subconscious, we decided early on that if anger equals pain, then the best way to keep from causing pain to others or incurring pain by others would be to bust a gut, get a migraine, numb our body and soul, and just try with all our might to never get angry.

The big question is: How's that working for you?

In my experience, not well.

Most human beings get mildly or massively angry at the very least once a week, if not more often. Yes, even nice people. It's *what they do with* that emotion that makes all the difference.

To recap, here's how anger relates to pain: *Healthy/constructive* anger has not, will not, and cannot cause pain; quite the opposite. If anger is expressed appropriately, it equals energy, intimacy, and peace of mind. But *unhealthy/destructive* anger is what causes everyone pain. The one experiencing and expressing destructive anger, and whoever is within the near vicinity of this contagious behavior, is going to feel small or serious amounts of pain.

The first step toward getting a grip on rage is to know what it is.

Chapter 2

Rage: The Real Culprit

P ain, violence, and punishment have nothing to do with constructive anger and everything to do with destructive anger—which is really a poor disguise for rage.

Rage is as different from anger as night is from day; as apples are from orangutans. Remember, anger is a feeling and emotion. Rage has the ability to cover other feelings, but it is not a feeling or emotion in itself. It is an *action* or *behavior* used to disconnect us from any and all emotions. Rage is a negative coping mechanism that numbs peoples' feelings.

Cocaine, alcohol, heroin, and sugar numb us. Too much of anything numbs us, too—too much television, too much time at the computer, too many hours at work; all are ways to numb our feelings.

Rage is like a huge dose of morphine. It is a drug that is legal, plentiful, readily available, and can be addictive.

Rage creates more rage. It is more contagious than the flu, cancer . . . or compassion. Rage spreads like the wildfires in California, destroying everything and everyone in its path. It is a huge factor in divorces, delinquency, and the dissolution of families, friendships between individuals, and business partnerships.

At fifty years old, Burt is prematurely gray but his face and body look like they belong to a man half his age. In my consultations with him he discovered—what many men I've worked with have—that when his construction company is making much less money than he needs, rather than feeling afraid or like a failure, he rages at his employees and even his own family members (especially his brother Bill, who is his on-site foreman). Burt realized that on the surface rage looks more potent and powerful than does being a scared businessman who shakes in fear when viewing the bottom line. To Burt, rage *feels* temporarily empowering, but here's the rub: It is only an illusion. Rage weakens both the person who is raging and the person who takes the brunt of the rage.

Sandra is an attractive stay-at-home mom who is sad and lonely most of the time because she is married to a workaholic, alcoholic husband. He is rarely home, but when he is, he's unbearable. Sandra refuses to sleep in the same bed with him and goes on retail therapy binges that maxed out their credit cards. Is this healthy anger? No, Sandra's actions are examples of rage. When I asked her if it was time she felt her anger and extricated herself from this painful partnership she actually said, "How can I get angry at him? He works hard for us and his drinking isn't really that bad." Not only could she not see how her rage was throwing them both into financial, not to mention emotional, ruin, she was in complete denial about having any anger, healthy or unhealthy.

If destructive anger is identified and understood, seen for what it is, and dealt with, all kinds of feelings, emotions, memories, hurts, slights, abandonments, and other issues that have been locked inside (perhaps for decades) will surface. Following, you'll find a list of traits and examples that further distinguish healthy anger from destructive rage.

How to Tell the Difference between Anger and Rage

A woman called me the other day for help. When I asked her what the problem was, she didn't hesitate: "I am living with the angriest man in the world."

I said, "Tell me how he expresses his anger."

After four or five descriptive sentences, I said, "I hate to interrupt, but everything you've said so far is *rage*." And she said, "What's the difference?"

Anger is about the "here and now"; it is a response to issues and situations occurring at the present time. You feel anger because of what your boss said to you this morning or because your spouse incorrectly balanced the checkbook this week.

Rage is about the "there and then"; it is about our past. Rage is a reaction to what your boss has said to you every morning for the last year. What you've stuffed and bottled up all this time, suddenly comes gushing out like a geyser. Likewise, rage occurs because the checkbook has gone unbalanced for two years, seemingly warranting a deafening silence to correct or punish your spouse's behavior. Rage can also be fueled by a seemingly over-and-done-with matter that has never really been resolved, such as being unable to trust a spouse who strayed once, years ago.

Anger lives in the present and so takes minutes, at the most, to be felt and expressed. It gets to the point and moves on. When Jerome's wife was late for a special luncheon they'd planned, Jerome said, "I'm angry. Now I only have forty-five minutes left for lunch before I have to return to work. Let's eat and make the most of our time."

Rage lives in the past and takes a very long time because it is grounded in our personal life history. Once it is unleashed, it wants to remain where it is, unresolved. In contrast with the above scenario, in a rage situation no one wants to eat with anyone because no one has an appetite left: When Sandy's chronically late boyfriend was late once again, her response was, "I'm tired of you always putting everything before me. Didn't your mother teach you it is rude to keep people waiting? I got here on time. I can't see why you can't!" . . . and she was just getting warmed up. Clearly, there was more than anger going on.

Rage is what constitutes most marathon arguments. You know, the ones that begin at eight o' clock after dinner after the kids are put to bed and that are still going strong at one in the morning until someone cries uncle and says, "Does anyone know the original point of this?" or attempts to just share some feelings.

HEALTHY ANGER	RAGE/UNHEALTHY ANGER
Is a feeling	Is a reaction
Is a primary emotion	Stifles or masks emotions
Is neither positive or negative	Is negative and inappropriate
Provides energy	Drains energy
Is meant to be given away	Is meant to be given up
Doesn't hurt anyone	Hurts everyone involved
Clears the air	Clouds communication
Increases understanding	Adds to confusion
Helps communication	Increases conflicts and misunderstandings
Rights injustices and wrongs	Is an injustice and wrongs people further
Increases intimacy and peace of mind	Creates or increases the distance between people and causes discord
Heals	Damages
Is contained and controlled until directed at the proper time, place, and/or person	Is pervasive, out of control, and misdirected
Concerns the present	Concerns the past
Is about "me"	Is about "you"

Anger is about "me" and rage is about "you": If I express anger, I am telling you about me, stating my immediate feelings. Anger is revealing. If I am raging, I'm telling you about you, rehashing your past behavior(s), and thus I am concealing what I am really feeling and going through right now.

Rage perpetuates when two parties use it habitually to avoid meaningful discussion. One spouse tells the other what he or she didn't do and shouldn't have done; why what he or she said or did is wrong, crazy, sick, or messed up; or that he or she "always" commits a perceived offense. When this party finally finishes the diatribe, then it's the other spouse's turn to tell the first how it is all that person's fault, and how what was said doesn't apply and "there you go again," and if the first speaker had only read more self-help books the words wouldn't have been said at all. After that, then it's the first speaker's turn again, and then the second, and we affectionately call this marriage and then very often we call it adversity or irreconcilable differences and grounds for divorce.

Rage has moved more people out of relationships than has U-Haul. It shoves everyone out the door, out of lives, or out of business. Rage pushes everyone away because no one wants to be around it.

On the other hand, anger expressed in present time and in an appropriate manner actually draws people to you. If a man says to his wife, "I'm angry and I need to talk," nine times out of ten the wife will respond with something like, "Okay, tell me more," or "I'm listening," or "What's going on?"

If an employee says to a fellow worker, "I'm angry about what went on in the staff meeting this morning," most fellow employees will say, "What's bothering you?" or "Let's talk about it this afternoon over a beer." In other words, if I do not rage at you, you have no reason to run—indeed, anger can create the beginning of many productive dialogues and initiate problem solving.

Rage engenders defensiveness, distance, and the feeling of being in some kind of danger; it shows disrespect and disregard for both the speaker and the one expected to listen. If your boss blows up at you during a meeting, then refuses to discuss the matter further even in private, this behavior basically says—in no uncertain terms—"I do not value you or this relationship enough to warrant an expenditure of my time or energy to try to achieve resolution." Anger, on the other hand, shows appreciation and respect, as well as a belief that the other person is able to respond with equal civility. If your boss is angry and says so and follows that statement with something like, "and I'd like for you to meet me for lunch so we can discuss the issue," this says, "I value you and our relationship enough to make some time and to request that you make some time to resolve the issue at hand."

Anger is a *response* to injustice, rudeness, impoliteness, impoverishment, impudence, and abuse. Rage is a *reaction* to situations, circumstances, people, processes, and problems.

Anger responses are generated by present stimuli and work toward resolving them. Rage reactions are a reactivation of one's history and memories about people, processes, and problems, blocking progress or resolution.

Angry responses are proportional to what is coming toward or being taken away from us. Rage reactions are almost always disproportionate to what is being said or done (or not said or done) to one's satisfaction.

Rage-reactive behaviors and actions warrant these types of reactions from others: "Where is all of this coming from?" or "Why are you making a mountain out of a molehill?" In other words, the person might have a pound's worth of basis for an angry discussion, but is dumping a ton's worth of rage on someone.

Rage incorporates statements like, "you always" or "you never." They often include ultimatums and threats. The one raging has a black-and-white mind-set, all or nothing, or my way or the highway.

Anger speaks in terms of "sometimes," "occasionally," and "every now and then." Anger is comfortable with some gray areas.

Anger engages with the genuine conflict, whereas rage runs from it, hurling obstacles in its path. Angry men or women are in essence saying, "I have a problem, and I am seeking a solution." People who are in a rage say, "*You* have/are a problem and *that's* the problem"—with no interest in working together toward a solution.

Anger says, "Let's confront these divisive issues without adding to them"; rage says, "Let's further divide." A CEO who attended one of my corporate anger presentations stood up during my talk and said, "I never run from confrontations. I stand toe to toe with anyone. I get in their face no matter what I have to do or say to get my point across." The sturdy, sixty-year-old with a crew cut sat down with a satisfied look on his face.

I responded, "Does that include yelling, calling people names, and other like behaviors or actions?"

"Whatever it takes!" he replied.

The actions and behaviors often employed in conflicted situations are self-defeating expressions of rage. One reason is that many people (including the aforementioned CEO) are actually feinting to avoid conflict, in spite of how things may appear on the surface. They hate confrontations because in the past this meant they felt defeated by their parents, coaches, teachers, partners, or former partners. They think a good defense is a good offense.

But perhaps a more significant explanation for so much avoidance is that most people have not been taught how to do it with a win-win attitude. Instead we're taught there can only be one winner or one loser, an approach grounded in rage.

When we realize that inappropriate reactions are ineffective, are merely covering our emotions *including our anger*, we develop a new freedom to speak our feelings—even those that express criticism or expose our vulnerability—without fear of retaliation and retribution. And now that our responses are proportional to people and circumstances, neither the speaker nor listener has anything to fear.

> ## WORDS USED BY THE RAGING PERSON:
>
> - You always _____
> - You never _____
> - Why can't you just _____
> - If only you _____
> - It's all your fault
> - Shame on you
> - You're lying
> - When are you going to _____

Soft Rage

We're not talking about road rage or domestic violence. This isn't putting your fist through a plate glass window, either. No, the kind of rage I am going to discuss now is what I call "soft rage." Soft rage is the kind of rage that has been called anger and that most people have seen, received, or perpetrated during all of their life. It is the rage (often viewed as anger) that is seen on television, movies, and the Internet and experienced in our homes and businesses. It is usually not intentional or malicious. It is the rage that is done more out of habit than to really harm. The forms of rage that will be discussed are complicated and I am going to make it as simple as possible. What you will see, however, is there is nothing "soft" about any of these.

Given so few people have ever seen or heard anger expressed appropriately, they go with what they have seen and heard a million times since childhood. Because rage is the norm, men and women have unintentionally cast themselves as both victims and perpetrators.

HOW TO IDENTIFY "SOFT RAGE"

Is your tone? . . .
- Patronizing
- Condescending
- "Holier than thou"
- Rude
- Sarcastic

The Five Things People Do When They Think They Are Expressing Healthy Discontent

Rage is a shape-shifter. It can come in the guise of some otherwise positive or appropriate behaviors. For example, if you are a teacher, it is perfectly appropriate to share your knowledge with your students. They are there to learn from you. But teaching can be used as a disguise for rage.

During one of my presentations to a group of CEOs, one very confident man leaned over to another and said, "Bud, you look like you're not getting this rage stuff. I can explain it to you during the break so it will be easier to grasp." The man who heard this looked at the speaker as if to say, "I didn't sign up to be your student or take your class. And I'll let you know if I need your help, thank you very much." If you impose upon another person what you think he or she should know, when the individual has not solicited your help, then that "teaching" becomes a subtle form of rage.

Judges sit in front of a courtroom to do just that—judge. That's their job, their function in our justice system. Conversely, it is not a mother's job to judge her grown daughter's boyfriends and classify her choices as "losers." This is rage.

These are all actions and behaviors used to numb people to their true feelings and emotions:

- Shaming
- Blaming
- Criticizing
- Preaching and teaching
- Judging

Shaming

Shaming is one of the most commonly used forms of rage. Shame comes from the Anglo-Saxon word *sceamu,* meaning "to cover." Many people have been covered in shame since childhood: "You are a disgrace to your family," said Bill to his gay son, Roger, during a counseling session. "You should be ashamed of yourself," says the wife of the alcoholic husband. "It is my job to put you to shame," says the fundamentalist preacher. "I can't believe someone as intelligent and well read and educated as you can't figure it out," said Tom's father to him, regarding Tom's failed relationship.

Shame is a psychological slap in the face to children and adults that is neither subtle nor soft.

Demeaning statements to induce shame may be made every few minutes when people are angry but can't feel or express their anger. Instead, words are selected to degrade and lower self-esteem. The father who is good with his hands says to the gangly, awkward twelve-year-old, "No matter how many

times I show you how to do this, you're never going to get it."
"What's wrong with you? Math is easy," says the math instructor who may be just as weak in some other subject (and may have been demeaned by another instructor in just such terms).

Disdain is one of the most destructive of all raging behaviors. Someone who is disdainful toward another writes that person off as worthless. The speaker makes plain he or she views the other person's character with contempt, scorning the listener's very existence. In that moment, it can crush a sensitive soul. "Your sister has all the brains in this family," the father said to his son.

Blaming

Blame is thrown around fast and furiously. Like a hard metal disk thrown with accuracy and precision, blame can take the head off a loved one. "If you had only gotten into therapy when I first asked you to, we wouldn't be in this mess we're in now," said the wife to her husband. Susan told her husband, Sam, during a workshop, "We can't afford a cabin in the woods, but you wouldn't listen. Now we may have to sell our real home and live with bears and bugs."

We blame our parents instead of holding them accountable. We blame our accountants for not being responsible. We even shame and blame ourselves for not going into counseling or not hiring the right accountants in the first place. Blaming someone else for our mistakes, failures, and general discontent is a way to abdicate responsibility for our lives and keeps us from feeling sad, angry, or hurt. Blaming is an action that finds fault without leaving open any avenue for mending.

Criticizing

The above statements are warning shots fired over the bough to let the listener know that what's coming next isn't going to feel good at best and may ruin his or her day or perhaps the entire decade.

Men and women have been using criticism to control, manipulate, coerce, get even, or just plain attack since the first *Homo erectus* uttered the words, "You're not really going *Tyrannosaurus rex* hunting dressed like that, are you?"

We've all been criticized so many times without soliciting it that it may be difficult for many of us to see it as an action or behavior that qualifies as rage. And yet I've had dozens of men, women, and adolescents in my office saying they have had it with the critic in the family or workplace that can never be satisfied and finds something wrong in everything they say or do. I'm talking about unsolicited critiques and comments that leave many, even thick-skinned, people feeling as if a knife has sliced through their spirit.

> ### CLASSIC CRITICIZING STATEMENTS:
> - "I'm just telling you for your own good . . . "
> - "I say this because I love you"
> - "With all due respect . . . "
> - "No disrespect intended . . . "
> - "I hope you won't take offense, but . . . "

The wife who says to her husband, "Do you like this dress?" is one thing—the husband who says, "You're not seriously thinking of going out dressed like *that*, are you?" has probably been gunny-sacking anger about something and has now crossed the line into rage.

Preaching and Teaching

Have you ever preached "the gospel according to you"? You know—the words that flew out of your mouth, trying to convert someone to your way of seeing things. Perhaps you've preached the detrimental effects of smoking, demonized hard drink or hard living, or simply that like Mark Twain said, "Golf is a good walk spoiled," to the sixty-two-hole-playing reprobate? Perhaps you've tried to convert a wayward husband to the values of psychotherapy or recovery?

Preaching is a form of rage when the one doing so is trying to hammer a point of view, interpretation, morality, or value into someone who is not seeking conversion. The preacher feels it is his or her duty, right, or obligation to get a sermon across whether we have asked for it or not, and in that resistance to listening is all the more justification that the sermon is necessary.

Again, don't get me wrong—if you attend a house of worship, you are expecting to hear preaching; but our spouse, children, aging parents, girlfriend/boyfriend, or employees didn't sign on to be members of our congregation in "The Church of I'm Right and You're Wrong."

The teaching form of this rage reaction is more covert than the preaching form. Teaching is one of the more subtle forms of rage because on the surface it appears to be really helpful. But if you go beneath the surface, you'll often find condescension, patronization, and belittling.

Teachers read self-help books with a trusty pink or yellow highlighter at the ready to underscore all the passages that pertain to their husband-student, girlfriend-student, or parent-student. Then they might leave the book open to the most pertinent page in the most inconspicuous places like, say, the bathroom sink or the other person's pillow.

Their student upon finding it might cry out, "Honey, did you want me to read this book lying in the sink marked with pink and yellow highlighter with my name in the margins?" Another important thing to note: When the frustrated or self-appointed preacher or teacher is engaged in these subtle forms of rage, it may not have anything to do with what the person to be instructed has recently said or done. These are merely ways to leak out or reassert rage that has been inside the speaker for days, weeks, or decades.

Judging

When people are angry but don't know how to express it appropriately, they very often fall back on a tactic that was probably used on them since childhood and they have become masters of in adulthood—judging. This form of raging requires that the individuals have an imaginary robe and a gavel handy at all times. They judge your behavior—the way you speak, stand, sit, eat, work, play, make love, buy groceries, make repairs, raise your children, tie your shoes, and so on.

Judges also get to play jury to decide guilt or innocence regarding the offenses they see you committing—"I sentence you
to the silent treatment for forty-eight hours," or "Off to rehab
for twenty-eight days," or "No sex for you for a month."

And sometimes these judges even get to be executioner for
the most serious blunders. They can issue a death sentence to
relationships, marriages, jobs, and especially self-esteem and
self-worth.

When couples or colleagues fight, it goes something like this:

"Here's what you did wrong. Here's what you should have
done/thought/said/said this way, instead of the way you
did/thought/ . . . "

A close cousin to being judged is being analyzed by someone
other than a therapist who was solicited and is being paid for
his or her services. This can be very annoying.

Picture this: The impudent husband looks at his wife with
a cold, clinical stare. She feels the heat-seeking missile of his
gaze into her psyche and finally she says, "Are you angry with
me?"

The husband strokes his wannabe Freudian chin, "Angry?
No, I'm not angry. You know I haven't had a real feeling since
the Nixon administration. No, what I'm trying to do is figure
you out, make some sense of your behavior, and come to an
understanding of why you think and behave the way you do.
After meeting your mother and father, I know where some of
your behavior is coming from . . . "

Or, "What were you thinking?" The irate father says to the
son who put a dent in the SUV. "What is wrong with you? Let's

---

MORE EXAMPLES OF RAGE

- Sarcasm
- Put-downs
- One-upmanship
- Sabotage
- Jokes (The kind of jokes where someone is the "butt" and is not laughing even though everyone in the room may think it is funny. If it is a funny joke, everyone laughs. If the speaker has to add at the end of a joke that it is a "joke," then it probably isn't.)
- Manipulation
- Control
- Lies
- Gossip

---

sit down and start from the beginning, so we can see how you came to be so . . . "

These analytical phrases imply that the speaker is the "doctor" and the listener is the "patient."

All five of the discontented behaviors and actions are serious, so serious that I have tried to add a touch of levity here and there to hopefully reduce the pain of recognizing how many times they have been done to you and you have done them to the ones you love.

All five result in distance, disaster, and very often divorce. All five must be eliminated from our conversations and confrontations.

I presented these five things to a group of social workers last week in a seminar on expressing anger appropriately. A man in his early forties raised his hand and with a slight whimsical tone asked, "If you take away these things, what in the world am I going to say? I say this stuff almost every day."

Four Styles of Rage

There are four predominant styles of rage. They are vehicles that deliver the five kinds of discontent right to your head, heart, and soul. All four are frequently used, but some people gravitate more to one or two styles. They are:

- The Interrogator
- The Intimidator
- The "Poor Me"
- The Distancer

The Interrogator

The interrogator is the rager who has *ways to make you talk.*

"What time did I tell you to be home?" "Who were you with?" "How many times have we had this conversation?" "How much did you have to drink?" "What is your excuse?" "How many times have I told you?" "When are you going to visit?" "Why don't you ever call?"

The interrogator employs a series of rapid questions to control, manipulate, shame, judge, and so on, leaving everyone exhausted and willing to sign any confession just to get out of the cold cement room with its one dim lightbulb and one-way mirror.

The Intimidator

The intimidator is the man or woman who rages by getting big and loud and filling up the entire room with a gigantic roar. This is done to demean and demoralize others and make them feel small and silent. The intimidator curses loudly and throws objects off tables or desks. He or she often employs preaching, sarcasm, and put-downs.

Sometimes an intimidator fills up the room with silence so thick you can cut it with a knife. Everyone around the potentially raging individual is whispering and walking on eggshells, hoping the intimidator won't "snap."

Intimidators believe "might makes right," and they're always going to have the last word.

The "Poor Me"

The "poor me" rager is just as full of rage as the others but does not have enough energy to question or get large. This person feels like the victim in every situation and uses complaining, justifying, draining language to get his or her demands or grievances across.

"Am I the only one who has to work around here? I clean up the house before going to work. I work all day long, fight the commute home, and when I get here the house is a mess again," say mothers (and sometimes fathers) everywhere.

"You'd think after working all day and putting up with all that I have to put up with I could come home and relax, but noooooooooooo!"

"I know I'm late for our lunch meeting," Jason said to his boss. "But just as I was getting ready to leave the office, this customer called and he just kept talking and talking and I knew you were going to be mad at me for being late again. But what could I do? I had to talk to him. So don't be angry at me. It's my customer's fault, not mine."

You know you're a "poor me" if you are often asked in a sarcastic tone, "Would you like some cheese with your whine?"

The Distancer

The distancer is the most prevalent style. The distancer has one foot in and one foot out of every conflict, confrontation, and argument.

This type uses one of the worst four-letter words in relationships; one that communicates nothing: F-I-N-E. Cherie says she hears this word from her husband all the time, as he tunes her out.

A distancer also uses the word *whatever* quite a bit. Both words basically say, "I'm out of here and you can do whatever you want and I'll say it's fine, but really it isn't fine at all." If someone wants to be a good distancer, he or she will put these two words together, in a tone of boredom or exasperation: "Fine! Whatever!"

The distancer is emotionally unavailable, shut down, and numb. He or she is "here" only in body, but is absent in every other sense.

Enraged or Outraged?

I have tried to make a distinction between what we normally think of and label as rage—hitting, slapping, pinching, pushing, or road rage—by calling the behaviors in this chapter "soft rage." I'm sure by now you see truthfully there is no such thing. All rage hurts everyone concerned. Most people tend toward being either enraged or outraged. Oddly enough, enragers tend to partner or marry outragers. Outragers try to get the enrager to ratchet up their behaviors whereas enragers try (sometimes for a lifetime) to tone outragers down.

Enragers tend to hold everything in, for days or even decades. They bottle up their emotions and try to put a lid on every feeling that is uncomfortable. They tend to stew, seethe, and get stressed out. They project their accumulated fears and rage onto others. Enragers often employ shame and criticism, and can be very harsh judges of others.

Outragers, on the other hand, *externalize* their fears instead of facing them. The homophobic enrager votes against gay marriage and won't associate with any gay people. A homophobic outrager will hurl epithets, slurs, and other outrageous comments.

YOU MIGHT BE AN **ENRAGER** IF YOU	YOU MIGHT BE AN **OUTRAGER** IF YOU
Stew and obsess	Yell or scream
Self-medicate with drugs, alcohol, food, sex, and so on	Throw things
Can't let go	Slam doors
Keep resentments	Break things
Fixate	Curse

RAGE IS . . .

- Hurtful
- Tied to the past
- Used to distract, distance, or dictate
- About "you," not "me"

Outragers tend to be active in their persecution of others who don't feel, think, believe, or behave like them. Outragers curse loudly, throw things, scream, and never lower their voice.

It's hard to say which of the two types are more dangerous to relationships.

Some of you may think that outrage can be a positive thing. For example, if someone is falsely accused of a crime, the public becomes "outraged" until the media gets involved forcing the city for a new trial where the defendant is found innocent and eventually set free. Sounds great, except for one thing: That's not outrage, because no one gets hurt. True outrage is more like a witch hunt that sends innocents to the stake.

Whether you find yourself or someone you know in either or both categories, take heart. You are about to be introduced to a tool that can help and even heal while turning both the enrager and outrager into a person who talks, acts, thinks, and feels like what indigenous cultures refer to as "human beings."

Chapter 3

Emotional Regression:
The Secret Behind Anger and Rage

E motional regression is one of the best-kept secrets in modern psychology. Virtually nothing is written on the subject,
or certainly very little that explains it and relates it to everyday
life, especially as it impacts on anger and rage. Emotional regression can be defined in many ways and you may be familiar
with the following ones because either you've employed them
recently or someone has said them to you:

- "I wish you'd grow up."
- "You're acting like a big baby."

Perhaps less common—but still a good way to define regression—is that it is an unconscious return to our past history.
When we regress, we are hurled into our past faster than light-
ning. We say things or react the way we did when we were in
our twenties, teens, or late or early childhood. This is not the

READING THE BODY FOR REGRESSION

The sensations below are all physical signs of regression:

Cold hands and feet	Trouble breathing
Perspiring excessively	Excessive drowsiness
Lump in throat	Clenched jaw
Heart beating wildly	Extreme headache
Knot in stomach	Hands shaking
Excessive dry mouth	Face and neck flushed
Tight chest	Dry mouth

same as consciously drawing on the past to solve a problem in the present by thinking back and remembering how we solved a similar issue earlier; rather, it is an unconscious and unintentional revisiting of deep feelings and reactions we felt at one time, which we now find ourselves reliving over and over.

The best example of this for many people is when they go home for the holidays. Approaching our parents' driveway, we're still feeling like an adult. Once we cross the front door threshold, Mom and Dad start talking or interacting with us as they did thirty years earlier. Before we know it, we're speaking to them—sometimes even saying word for word what we had said back then—as if we were twelve or thirteen.

Sharon says every time she goes home for a visit, it isn't long before the regressive behavior begins. Her mother, who is in her midseventies, starts commenting about her clothes or hair. Sharon says, "My mom gives me a warm hug, then steps back and gently brushes my hair back and says the same thing: 'Honey, why don't you get your hair out of your face? You have such a pretty face. People want to see your beautiful face.' I want to ignore her but instead I say, 'Mom, it's my hair and my face and I'll wear it any way I want to.' I'm forty-four years old, for God's sake. When does it stop?"

Bob says, "Every time I go home, my father will say something like, 'Son, when are you going to get a real job and settle down and make some good money? You know you can always come to work for me.' I keep telling him, 'Look, Dad, it's my life,' but I never say I'll be retiring from teaching college in two years."

Another good place to see regression in action is at the grocery store. While shopping a few months ago, I caught the tail end of an exchange between a mother in her midthirties and her daughter who must have been three or perhaps four. The mother, who looked exhausted and frazzled, was pushing the cart through the aisle and her daughter was in the seat looking at her. The little girl put her fingers in her ears and wagged them and stuck out her tongue and said to her mother, "I'm mad at you and I'm not going to talk to you anymore!" Within a nanosecond, the mother put her fingers in her ears and stuck out her tongue and said, "Well, I'm mad at you and I'm not going to talk to you anymore, either." I thought, "Who is going to drive them home? They are both four, for goodness' sake." The mother wasn't kidding. She was raging and regressing.

So the truth is, if your parents don't make you regress, your children sure can.

Another and more recognizable way to think about regression is when a full-grown adult feels small or little. This happens when men and women feel as if they've lost their age and maturity and feel six inches tall instead of six feet, or feel like a four-year-old instead of a forty-year-old. Recently on the *New York Times* best-seller list was a wonderful, heartfelt memoir, *Chosen by a Horse*, by Susan Richards. She writes about having to put down her beloved equine companion that she'd rescued from an abusive owner eighteen years before. When it came time to do this heartbreaking task, Richards most assuredly felt deep anger and sadness and wrote, "I wish some grown-up could have come in and made the decision for me." At the time, she was sixty-five years old going on twelve or less. She felt small and anything but like a powerful, competent adult.

Charles says, "Every time anyone looks at me in a certain way (which I can't even explain), I just want to scream at them, 'What the hell are you looking at?' I think it's the way I felt when I had a real bad case of acne at around fifteen or sixteen. I hated those years but even more I hated the way people looked at me."

I have counseled many doctors, surgeons, and even nurses who have experienced rage and regression after losing a patient. When I asked them to describe how they felt, they said almost exactly the same thing—that they felt "little" or "small" and as if they were frauds or actors playing a role they were not prepared for. This feeling of being small or little comes to all of us no matter how powerful, successful, rich, or poor we are, and it doesn't feel good.

Another way to think about emotional regression is illustrated best by the words many of us have said and heard—"I lost it!" or "I lost my temper."

Jamie said to me in a session, "Yesterday my husband, Todd, and I were having this very frank, honest, even refreshing conversation and I don't know what he said, but *I lost it.* I started screaming at him all of a sudden and couldn't stop myself. He finally stormed out of the house and didn't come back for hours. What is that about? That wasn't my first temper tantrum, either."

"I found marijuana in my son's chest of drawers," said Thomas. "And I don't know what happened but *I lost it.* When he came home from school, I yelled at him for two solid hours. I grilled him the way my father did when I was his age. We haven't spoken two words since. Here's the weird thing: I smoked grass at his age and swore if I ever caught my children doing it, I'd approach it maturely, sanely, and rationally. I was screaming my head off at him."

What do mature adults lose at these critical moments? Lots of things, including logic, reason, rationality, maturity, and the ability to choose their words carefully and considerately. They lose their perspective, balance, and, most of all, their ability to stay in the prefrontal portion of their neocortex.

When people lose it, when they feel small, little, or less than the powerful person they are most of the time and return to their past unintentionally, it may be explained not only emotionally but neurologically and biochemically as well.

The Brain and Regression

The amygdala might be called the "little memory that keeps us safe" portion of the brain. In other words, this almond-shaped portion of the brain, located near your temples, remembers that thirty years ago someone in a black coat screamed at you and scared you to death. Thirty years later, you see a man in a black coat coming toward you and you feel two inches tall and want to run and hide even though you don't know the person and they haven't said a word.

When he was twelve, as Ben shared with me one day during a session, his math teacher spontaneously called on him to come to the front of the room and solve a problem on the chalkboard. What she didn't know—couldn't have known—was that Ben had a full erection from staring at Sharon Bennington all during the class. The teacher kept tapping the chalk on the board, repeating his name over and over. "Every time she tapped that board and called my name, my erection got bigger and bigger and I wanted to disappear. I finally went up there and everyone in the class saw it and laughed and to this very day if someone is tapping or calling my name in a certain way, I become that twelve-year-old boy that was frustrated and full of rage at being singled out and embarrassed to death."

When we lose it, we leave the neocortex (the most recently developed, outer layer of the brain) and head straight for the oldest part—the reptilian brain. This portion of the brain is only capable of notifying us when to eat, excrete, procreate, fight, flight, or freeze—no logic, no reason, no choice—just the basic survival abilities. The reptilian brain can't choose to express anger appropriately; it can only rage.

Here's the key: when we regress we go into fight mode—not with clubs like our ancestors, but with hard words and even harsher silence. Or we run away, fly away, drive away, and get the hell out of there. If we can't fly or fight, we freeze like the gazelle that can't outrun or overcome the faster cheetah. We freeze in dead marriages for thirty or forty years or in dead-end jobs until retirement. We wait until the danger has passed, the divorce is final, or the predator finds something else to chase. All of these are regressive reactions and all are forms of rage.

Emotional regression, then, is not a neurosis or psychosis. It can't be cured once and for all because it is simply a part of the human condition. However, we can identify and catch our regressions and train ourselves to come out of them and back into the present to our job, marriage, friendships, and family. The faster this happens, the better, since regressions usually equal regret. When we say something, not say something, do something, or not do something while in a regressed state, the repercussions may last for hours, days, or even decades. When we can only fight, fly, or freeze with those we love, care about, or work with and not make choices based on logic, reason, and the ability to respond proportionately, the pain we create can sometimes be unbearable and too often unforgivable. Therefore, we need to develop skills to head off regression at the pass.

Emotional Regression:
A "Present-Person/People Eraser"

Another powerful way to think about emotional regression is that it is a present-person/people eraser. When Adrian and his wife, Sandra, argue, "She throws things; her purse, pillows, nothing hard, and she doesn't throw them at me, but it's like I see my father who did throw things at me when he was mad. He hurt me several times. I got a black eye once. I turn this five-foot two-inch, ninety-pound wife who wouldn't hurt a fly into a six foot, two-hundred-pound dad from forty-some years ago," he said during a session about his fears of anger and rage. Adrian's regression caused Sandra to disappear, and his father to come back out of the past.

Lonnie and Ramiro have been friends for twenty years. They worked at the same farm equipment sales office for as long as they've been friends.

"Two weeks ago I told Ramiro some personal stuff and I asked him to swear to never tell any of the people we work with." Lonnie paused and took a deep breath, "And that son-of-a-bitch blurted it out yesterday after work when a bunch of us met at a local bar. He'd had a few too many but I swear I want to kill him."

Long story short, Lonnie caught his regression and saw that his reaction was disproportional and realized he'd turned his close friend not only into an enemy but his mother.

"When I was nine, I stole some eight-track tapes from a music store. I remember asking my mother not to tell my dad who was out of town working. She promised she wouldn't and didn't for about two or three weeks. But one day she told him and he gave me the worst whipping of my life. I never trusted her again and, to be honest, I've always had a hard time trusting people for fear they'll betray me ultimately. I realize I turned Ramiro into Mom and that he'd just made a simple mistake, and I know when I bring it up I'm sure he'll say he's sorry and we'll be fine."

"You're just like my first husband" . . . "You are all alike" . . . "All women lie" . . . "All men cheat" . . . "You're just like the other therapist." These phrases suggest present-person/people erasing, meaning that the human being in front of someone who is angry is replaced with someone from his or her past, which causes rage. When someone's past is triggered, the typical reaction is to vent upon the one who evoked the emotional memory, or to seek solace in a regressive fashion.

When Jackie's husband left her, she said, "The first thing I did was call my mother, that's how regressed I was. My mother didn't finish calling him names before saying, 'I told you when I met Jimmy that he wasn't any good for you and that you could have done much better. Maybe you'll listen to your mother next time.' I felt about two years old. When she got through berating my husband, who by the way came back and we eventually worked everything out, I was looking for a womb to crawl into and more enraged with her than when I was with him."

The things people do when they think they are expressing anger—shaming, blaming, disdaining, put-downs, sarcasm, and so on, can trigger regressions in those who are on both the sending and receiving ends of such verbally abusive raging.

EXERCISE

On a scale of 1 to 5, circle the actions that very often trigger a regression by making you feel small, little, less than the powerful adult you are, or by making you lose it.

Shaming	1	2	3	4	5
Blaming	1	2	3	4	5
Criticizing	1	2	3	4	5
Preaching	1	2	3	4	5
Teaching	1	2	3	4	5
Judging	1	2	3	4	5
Analyzing	1	2	3	4	5
Sarcasm	1	2	3	4	5
Put-downs	1	2	3	4	5
Jokes at other's expense	1	2	3	4	5
Sabotage	1	2	3	4	5
Control	1	2	3	4	5
Manipulation	1	2	3	4	5
Lies	1	2	3	4	5
Gossip	1	2	3	4	5
One-upsmanship	1	2	3	4	5

The previous pages have provided you with real case histories that illustrate the different forms regression and the accompanying rage can take. Look at the following list and find the triggers for your own regressions, and then use this information to help catch yourself from falling into regression.

Now, look at the terms for which you checked 4s and 5s. When those buttons are pushed, how old do you feel? In other words, if you circled a 4 or 5 for "criticism" or "sarcasm," what age in your life do these take you back to?

Before we can understand other people's triggers for regression, we must first identity our own. Self-awareness always increases our empathetic abilities.

If Suzanne gets too much criticism, especially from her husband, Ronnie, she says, "I feel twelve years old." Ronnie reports that if he feels shamed, "It makes me feel five years old." Guess what Suzanne does to Ronnie when she's angry but can't express it appropriately to her husband, without shaming him? You guessed it! Ronnie childishly ups his criticism and rolls right over his wife. The results—a twelve-year-old and a five-year-old try to communicate and make decisions, and end up sleeping in separate rooms.

If you don't remember anything else about regression, I hope you'll take away this: Regression loves company. If Suzanne is going back to being an adolescent, she's going to take someone back in time with her.

There are three directions people can take when they find themselves or the person they are with is regressing: (1) The mature adult who is expressing anger appropriately can encourage and draw the other person out of his or her rage and regression; (2) the regressed one can pull the adult down into a raging regressed state of his or her own; and finally, (3) the adult won't go down and the regressed won't rise, so the two may have to go their separate ways for an hour, a day, a week, or perhaps forever.

Three Directions of Relationships and Regression

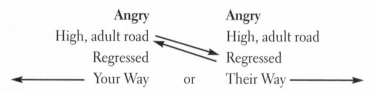

Angry
High, adult road
Regressed
←————— Your Way

or

Angry
High, adult road
Regressed
Their Way ————→

Other Potential Regressors
Too Much

One of the signs of a healthy adult is that the person's life is balanced. The search for balance is like the search for the Holy Grail. It is difficult at best and impossible at worst.

We've all heard the phrase, "Too much of a good thing." For many, "too much" is one of the triggers of emotional regression. Too much of nearly anything is fertile ground for the seeds of regression to burst into full bloom.

All work and no play makes Jack, Jill, or Bertha a dull, regressed, and sometimes raging person. Too much money can make one regress. Before you balk at that statement, think of the history and statistics of lottery winners. Fifty percent of those winners are in worse financial shape two years after winning than they were prior to holding the magic numbers. But even if you aren't cursed with the problem of excess work or money, you have probably experienced too much talking or stimulation or food. When you get out of balance and overindulge in anything, even anything pleasant, you will pay the price—regression.

Too much criticism, blaming, preaching, or teaching can turn an adult into a raging, tantrum-throwing child. You may know people at work or home who feel overwhelmed, resentful, and enraged when you give them too much attention or information, or this may be your reaction toward them if they touch one of your regression buttons.

Too Little

The other very popular regression producer is "too little." Again a well-known phrase, "too little, too late," comes to mind. All the things that regress people when they are given them in excess can just easily regress others if they aren't given enough. The lack or small amount of anything—such as food, touch, attention, tenderness, sex, rest, solitude, or companionship— can transfer people right back to the past, when they were deficient in these things.

Ever try to get something done when you're hungry or exhausted? Even if you continue to work, what you produce is usually subpar and will look like a jumbled mess once you've had a good night's sleep and some nutritious food. Our body, mind, and psyche need order and balance to function properly.

This deprivation keeps you regressed until you balance things out.

Think back to the children's story of Goldilocks and the three bears. This is a remedial way of teaching about regression and how children and grown-ups must find out what is "just right" for them. A job that is too big can repel us from wanting to deal with the present; a job that does not stimulate us makes us tune out also. A too-long visit with our parents leaves us wanting a blanky and a bottle; visits that are too infrequent and too short make us long to lie down in a short bed of regression, desiring to be nurtured.

Certain Looks

Everyone has seen the "look of love," but looks can exude less than happy vibes. Even the way someone looks at you can trigger a regression. The amygdala remembers only rough, raw details to keep us safe. A particular look a woman gives a man may be misinterpreted and misconstrued and illicit the phrase, "Why are you looking at me like that?" She might respond, "Like what?" And if he were not regressed he might say, "Like the look the father gave me when he wanted to punish me," or "A football coach in junior high," or "My mother." This part of the brain doesn't remember the details as to whether the perceived threat, real or imagined, came from a man or woman, it only records the facial expression.

Certain Sounds

Randy almost disappears into thin air every time he hears a fire truck's siren. "I can't help it. That sound scares me to death.

When I was seven, our house burned to the ground and we barely got out alive. Now, no matter where I am, if I hear the siren, I go right back to that moment even though the fire was over fifty years ago."

One afternoon in a couples session with Julie and Rachel, they shared with each other things that made each angry and frustrated. Suddenly Julie said to Rachel, "Why are taking that tone of voice with me?" Ultimately, we discovered it was a similar tone her ex-husband would take many times during their marriage.

Advertising counts on our nostalgic regressions every day. There is almost nothing that can be sold that is not tied to songs of my generation—baby boomers. Whether it's cars or soap, some song is played from the sixties in the hope that we'll all take a little trip down memory lane (which happens to be a cul-de-sac) and relive a pleasurable event or feeling. When advertisers associate that past good feeling with a present product, they've got a sale. We buy it and into it before becoming enraged at the fact that we didn't need what we bought or already had two just like it in a box we haven't opened.

Body Language

Experts and researchers in body language report that 85 to 95 percent of all communication is nonverbal. So no matter how many foreign languages we master, the body speaks louder and more precisely than our words.

A shaken finger at the wrong moment can send a person back to sitting in an uncomfortable pew listening to a pastor pointing out how the individual has failed or sinned. The crossing of arms, hands on hips, pursed lips, or the drumming of the fingers on a table can all become temporary time-traveling devices that lead us back to the anger and rage we couldn't show or articulate at the time.

One time in Chicago, I was giving a workshop on anger, rage, and regression. It was experiential, which means I had participants voluntarily come up front to do some work around a variety of issues. At one point I patted an empty chair that sat beside me, saying, "Who would like to come up here and deal with something that triggers your regression?"

I saw a man in the back of the room fidget in his seat. I patted the seat again a few more times. The man's face became red and flushed. Finally I patted it for a third time and said to the man, "Is there something coming up for you that you would like to deal with?"

"I guess so, because every time you pat that chair I want to leave the room. I keep hearing my mother patting her knees saying, 'Come on up here, Sonny, and give Momma a kiss. Momma's awful lonely,' and the more you pat, the angrier I get."

Going back to what I said earlier, what regresses one person means nothing to another. No one else in the seminar of fifty people was triggered by that seemingly innocuous patting, but for him it almost made him leave the workshop, totally enraged.

Dick is a slightly built man who weighs about 150 pounds and stands five feet seven inches tall. After attending the lecture in Asheville, North Carolina, he said he understood for the first time how he almost got in a fight at a bar a few months earlier with a guy twice his size and weight.

"A buddy of mine and I were having a beer as this guy walked into the bar. I'd never seen him before in my life. I leaned over to my friend and said, 'I'd like to go and kick that man's ass.' My buddy looked at me like I was crazy and I guess for a few moments I was. My friend said, 'That guy will kill you. Are you nuts? Do you know that guy?' The longer I looked at this guy, the angrier I got. Now I know it was rage. I wanted to fight this stranger. During this lecture I realized that guy reminded me of this bully in junior high school, who beat me up not only badly, but in front of dozens of my classmates. I've always hated that guy. This guy in present time has a haircut like my school nemesis and sort of stood real cocky like my bully. That guy would've killed me."

Words

Certain words trigger regressions. During a couple's session, Sam told his wife, Luanne, that when they would fight and she'd say before walking away, "I hate you!" he would lose it every time and want to get in his car and never come back. "I don't know what it is about those words that make me feel about five years old. They scare me to death."

After Luanne took a break, I asked Sam to try to remember where he'd heard those words before. What he discovered was emotional memories that had been buried alive in him for decades. When his father and mother fought what he called knock-down, drag-out fights, just as his father would leave to not come back for a time, sometimes his mother would say, "I hate you!"

"Every time Luanne says those words, she becomes my mom and I become a little boy wondering if and when I'll ever see my father again."

When Luanne returned, Sam told her about his parents' fights and about the words his mother used. Luanne cried and said she didn't know this and that she would promise to try to never say those words again, that she was sad that he had to hear those painful words as a child. They fell into each other's arms and wept.

Preconditions for Regression

There are five physical, psychological, and emotional states that, if avoided, will minimize the number of times and tendencies to regress, feel small, or lose it. I often point out that these states are not only common but really a part of almost everyone's personal and professional life. Many businesses such as Google spend time and energy reducing these preconditions in their workplace and that is part of the reason they receive over four thousand applications per day.

The preconditions are:

- Exhaustion
- Hunger
- Stress
- Illness
- Pressure

Exhaustion

Mental or physical exhaustion greatly increases one's time in the past. Extreme tiredness can make a grown man or woman yearn for care-free college days or a perpetual extended beach vacation. Exhaustion can take us out of the prefrontal, rational neocortex and send us to the preverbal state of the reptilian brain, to want to curl up and take a long, winter's nap.

Exhaustion makes us more susceptible to verbal, emotional, or physical abuse from our children, or bosses, parents, or other people in authority. It makes our skin paper thin and we tend to lose our ability to say such things as, "No," "No more," "Enough," or "Stop." We lack the necessary energy to take care of ourselves and then we become more likely to engage in co-dependent relationships, hoping to be rescued or saved for our ultimate well-being.

When we're tired, we can't think about the big picture. We seek things that are good for us for short-term, temporary fixes. We tend to settle for much less than we want or deserve in personal or professional situations and even relationships. We have a "short fuse"; we're grouchy, irritable, impatient, and impractical. We say and do things we may regret for years to come. We rage at the too-slow lady in front of us at the store checkout line and swear at a photocopier that runs out of paper.

Hunger

When a person has gone too long without food—there's that word again: *too*—the brain loses oxygen and blood flow. That,

in turn, leads to a lack of self-soothing chemicals such as serotonin, neo-epinephrine and oxytocin. Extreme hunger makes
us lose our patience, poise, and practicality. Hunger takes us
back to infancy as quickly as anything can. Once a person's
blood sugar is significantly altered, we yell at a spouse when
supper is not served on time much as we did in the crib at our
mother when nourishment was slow in coming. Adults who are
very hungry watch the second hand on their watch to see if the
waitress indeed comes to their table in "a minute" after seating
them. We may swear at the waitstaff as if they were slaves instead of servers.

Stress

Stress increases distress. When people are distressed, they become tense. Tension leads to contraction of body, mind, and
soul. Contraction creates rigidity, narrowness of mind and heart.
When people are stressed and in distress, you can give them
suggestions, advice, feedback, counseling, books to read, counselors to see, and none of it is taken in. All roll right off the
stressed, regressed individuals like water off a duck's back, and
they often even feel offended, letting you know it in no uncertain terms by raging.

What comes out of stressed, distressed people usually doesn't
make much sense. It usually lacks coherency, and continuity;
conversations are convoluted and confusing at best.

Now for the bad news—as if the above wasn't bad enough—
when we hear the word *stress*, we immediately think, "Welcome

to the American workplace," where stress has become the norm. Americans are working harder and longer and with less vacation time than ever. Cost of living rises while jobs are scarce and salaries decline. Work is outsourced to other countries. The average American worker is scared, exhausted, disconnected . . . and regressed.

The other negative quote we hear in our head about stress is, "Welcome to the average American home." Both parents are working, trying to make ends meet. Children have less supervision and interaction with parents, particularly the father. Studies show on average fathers spend less than two hours per week with their children. More and more children are being raised in one-parent homes. In much of the Western world, divorce occurs in one out of two marriages. All of these factors come together to produce stress, distress, and more and more regression, more and more unabated rage.

Illness

Minor or major illness will turn a grown man or woman into a big baby who wants to curl up and be fed and read to. Don't get me wrong, there's not a thing wrong with this. It's just that when illness strikes maturity, rationality, reasonability, sound judgment, and decision making go right out the door of the sickroom. Instead of requesting nurturing and comfort, we actually go into work anyway or refuse to go see the doctor. We want to deny our condition or have someone come take care of us, but we don't ask.

When people are sick, they kick into survival mode thinking, behaving, speaking, and listening. Now, put these all together and you end up with adults feeling pressured.

Pressure

Pressure to perform, pressure to please, pressure to achieve—pressure to be or not to be. While that may be the perennial question, the answer is pressure causes regression. Remove the pressure and you no longer feel as if you are an awkward adolescent or a stumbling toddler who can barely walk—let alone speak coherent, intelligent sentences.

Pressure leaves adults exhausted. Pressure causes or increases stress. Pressure makes us forget to eat or rest as we wrestle with real or imaginary deadlines. Enough pressure exerted long enough on coal turns it into a diamond. Too much pressure on people turns them into regressed, raging lumps too tense or exhausted to move.

Signs of Regression

Remember, different things regress people differently, but there are a few almost universal signs and signals that we are heading into our past history. You can never cure regression but you can learn to pick up on your particular triggers for regression. Once these are recognized, you can catch yourself before descending into the past or becoming the incredible shrinking man or woman. These signals are for both the one triggering the regression and the one who is feeling regressed. They are:

- Story Time
- Child Time
- Having disproportional energy
- Believing there is no choice
- Not talking enough
- Talking yet not saying anything
- Thinking you know best
- Can't ask for help
- The Triangle Tangle

Story Time

Story Time is when you torment yourself with possible negative scenarios.

Here's an example: John is a boss who is experiencing his own regression. On Friday afternoon, he says to his employee, Alex, "I want to see you in my office first thing Monday morning." What does Alex do? If statements like John's trigger an emotional memory like the one Alex has of his mother saying something like, "Wait until your father gets home" or "The principal is out today but he will deal with you Wednesday," Alex will begin Story Time. All weekend long, he will make up stories about what the John wants to talk about. Perhaps it was the fax paper he took home? No, wait. It was the personal charges made on the corporate card, or maybe worse—termination. With each worst-case scenario, Alex gets angrier and angrier and then finally settles into rage. No one in the history of employment has ever made up the story, "Hey, I bet he wants to talk about that raise I so readily deserve." When Alex exhausts all possible stories and gets to John's office, he is exhausted and feeling about five inches tall.

This chart breaks it down:

REGRESSED BOSS	EMPLOYEE— REGRESSED REACTION	EMPLOYEE— ADULT RESPONSE
Says, "I want to see you in my office first thing Monday morning," and nothing else.	Thinks, "I'm going to be fired!" then spends all weekend obsessing and creating worst-case scenarios. He comes to work on Monday upset, stressed, and feeling inadequate.	Thinks, "Maybe this is about the Smith account or maybe I'm going to get a raise. But since he didn't give me any more information, I'll just wait until Monday and I won't worry about it."
Says, "I want to see you in my office first thing Monday morning about the Smith account."	Thinks, "He must have hated the proposal I gave him on Smith. He's going to tear into me on Monday!" then spends all weekend freaking out and bad-mouthing his boss.	Thinks, "Great, I'll prepare the files and be ready on Monday," then doesn't worry about it on the weekend and has the information he needs on Monday.

When we regress, we almost always create worst-case scenarios. Interestingly, these fictitious stories from the regressed mind are a way to calm our fears, to self-soothe, but this attempt backfires and the result is more anxiety, not less. Ironically, such stories only increase our fear, anger, rage, and regression because they are appearing in living color from that part of the brain that is illogical and irrational. These semiparanoid parables can become quite extreme, ranging from the temporary belief that someone is plotting to punish you or control you, to the person's wishing to totally annihilate you.

Cheri is a stay-at-home mother. Twice divorced, she has trouble trusting her current husband. Her first husband died in a car crash and her second one cheated on her with another woman. Although she has worked on her anger and grief, she doesn't quite trust that Thomas, who she says is a fine man, will not eventually leave her.

Thomas had to go to Chicago on a business trip. He told her he would be in his hotel no later than ten and would call her no later than ten thirty. Cheri waited by the phone like a teenager waiting for her first crush to call. Ten thirty came—no call, ten thirty-five—still no call. Cheri has had a good deal of therapy so she didn't regress until ten forty.

"I wanted to know where he was. I bounced between anger, rage, and fear like a tennis ball. I started thinking something bad had happened to him; perhaps a car accident or the plane went down. I couldn't stop the terrible pictures that flashed through my mind as I waited for him to call. I saw him lying helpless or maybe dead in some ditch somewhere or in an emergency room. I was panicking. Then all of a sudden I pictured him with his secretary who went with him to that meeting and I thought that son-of-a-bitch had better be dead in a ditch because if I catch him with his secretary, I am going to kill him!" She was crying and laughing at the same time as she told me this story.

If no one in your life has ever wrecked a car, been taken to the emergency room, or cheated on you, then you say to yourself in situations similar to Cheri's, "I guess the plane was delayed and I'm sure he is all right and will call in the morning." You turn out the light and sleep like a baby, and by "like a baby" I don't mean you wake up every hour screaming and crying wondering where your mommy is. No—you sleep like an adult who is not triggered into dreaming up worse-case scenarios.

Where does the superability to concoct such dramatic and traumatic scenarios and stories come from? The answer is childhood. Who are the greatest storytellers in the world until they are talked out of, scolded, or punished out of their fantastic, creative abilities? Children. This natural storytelling ability is latent and comes back during such distressing times. Except now adults know "the ways of the world," so the stories seldom have happy endings.

Child Time

A four-year-old says to his or her mom or dad, "When are we going to go see Grandma?" The child's feeling of excitement and expectation turns into desperation when the parent replies, "In two weeks." Two weeks is an eternity for children.

You may recall how summers lasted forever and Christmas never came.

That four-year-old, forty years later goes to the doctor on Monday because of some condition that produces concern and anxiety. The doctor speeds in, performs a quick checkup, and on his way out says, "We'll have these tests back on Friday; try not to worry." Monday to Friday feels how long? Like an eternity. It is almost exactly the same feeling that children have, because the adult has regressed and is back in Child Time, which is full of worse-case scenarios.

When men and women regress, time gets weird. Regression leads to time's being compressed or expanded to becoming more dreamlike. Minutes feel like hours, hours feel like days, days seem like months, and months—well, months can become years.

For the son or daughter who hears, "Wait until your father gets home," time stands still. In the giddy fifteen-year-old waiting for her first date to show up, time is stuck in molasses. The wife waiting for the husband to call from his hotel feels as if time actually wounds her heart and soul, because she relives her first husband's cheating on her.

When we regress, time also contracts. If you are newly in love or remember being newly in love, you may recall that time collapsed in on itself. We leave adult time and descend into that oceanic oneness we experienced in the womb, or at our mother's breast. People very newly in love experience time so differently. The lover says, "Honey, I have to go out of town on a business trip." The other responds with a sad, perplexed tone,

"For how long?" "Three days," he reluctantly admits. "Three days! Three *whole* days? You have to quit your job. I can't live without you for three eternal days."

When we are in this state of bliss, we begin conversations with our loved one at 8:00 p.m. only to come out of the ecstatic trance at 2:00 a.m. with one of us saying something like, "Can you believe what time it is? We have been talking for six hours. Where did the time go?"

Same couple, ten years later . . . The wife says to the husband, "Honey, we need to talk." The husband is immediately on guard and responds spontaneously, "For how long?" "Oh just thirty minutes or so," she says. "Thirty minutes," the husband equates this to dog years, regresses, and says something like, "And I suppose you want me to listen the whole time."

During regression, time gets weird. When time is no longer "real," people tend to feel nervous and fearful, which then exacerbates regression, which then can lead to anger when the loved one doesn't call as promised. The good news is, once you know Child Time to be a sign of regression, you catch it and bring time back to its normal pace and thus reduce your anxiety and fear. This is a tool you didn't have to work with before.

Having Disproportional Energy

Although I've mentioned this sign of regression before, I feel it is important not only to include it on the list but also to explain the word *disproportional* and apply it to our sometimes disappointing conversations. I'm sure you have either said or heard someone say to you, "Where is all of this coming from?"—"this" being excessive energy about the problem or issue being discussed. The disproportional amount of energy feels overwhelming for many and just plain scary for others.

Those on the receiving end often feel they are being flooded by the speaker's words that comprise unfair accusations, insinuations, and criticism. This torrent of energy is not usually expressing enthusiasm; rather, judgment and shame. Therefore, listeners tend to feel pushed away or want to run away. But most of all, they feel confused. "Why is he talking to me this way?" Jill asked me one day during a consultation. "It's like he's talking to someone else and he doesn't even see me. Sometimes I think he's shouting at his first wife or his mother." I asked her how this made her feel. "Scared and angry. It pushed all my buttons and I feel like a little girl back in my parent's house, where I never felt seen, either."

When regressed people react disproportionally to an event, problem, or person, it is always about their history. And no one likes to have another person's history dumped into his or her lap or heart. We all have enough painful memories of our own. Now, don't get me wrong, I am open and receptive to hear your issues with me if we both are in the present; in other words, if I am not regressing, myself. But even when listeners are not regressed, they often will be after being hit with a barrage of hurtful words.

It is a fact that our body is a storehouse of wisdom, knowledge, feelings, and memories. As the poet Tim Sibles says in his poem "The Body Knew," "Long before there were words . . . the body knew." We've all had a "gut feeling" or a sense that something "doesn't feel right." Well, paying attention to our own body can help us detect when we are going into a regression that may lead to raging and be another useful tool to catch us going into a regressed place.

If at the mere thought of having an important conversation that will be very stressful, critical, and perhaps crucial your hands or feet become sheets of ice, chances are that you are regressing and going back to a time where and when a conversation of equally extreme importance took place. The body remembers that conversation didn't yield a positive result. Or perhaps it remembers that a particular dialogue should have taken place but didn't.

Every time Reginald thought about having that "father and son" talk with his fourteen-year-old about the dreaded subject of sex, he said, "I get a knot right in the pit of my stomach the size of a bowling ball." When I asked him how that same conversation went with his own father, he quickly answered without hesitation, "Terrible. It was so awkward and, besides, my dad sounded like an idiot. He didn't know any more about sex than I did, if what he told me was the extent of his own knowledge. I don't want to look like an idiot to my son but, like my dad, I don't really know what to say, either."

Traci and Doug came to see me for couple's counseling. They had been together for twenty years, since high school, but were having trouble really asking each other for what they wanted during lovemaking. Traci and Doug both have PhDs in psychology and biochemistry, respectively, but when it came time to talk about sex, Traci's neck and face flushed, turning fire engine red, and Doug reported that his heart was about to leap out of his chest and he'd feel a risk of rage at the thought of having to have such a connection in the first place.

Traci said, "We're educated adults and yet every time this whole thing is brought up, I feel like an adolescent." Doug added, "I don't even feel that old. I feel more like a six-year-old and this knot feels like it has been in my stomach forever."

Perhaps, like many, when called on to give a presentation of any kind, your mouth turns to cotton. No matter how much liquid you consume, your mouth is dry and the words won't be as fluid as you would like. Or maybe you get up to make the presentation and water is pouring out of every pore in your body. The room where you're speaking is a cool sixty-five degrees, but your shirt, blouse, or suit is soaking wet and you feel as hot as the Sahara desert. You are going back in time to a place where you didn't do too well with public speaking. Perhaps you were mocked, ridiculed, rejected, shamed, or given a bad grade. Or you declared yourself an unfit, inept speaker and have thought so ever since.

These knots, dry mouth, and excessive perspiration are more about your past than your present. Although many people have asked the question, "Couldn't these all be just signs of nervousness or anxiety?" in my experience, the answer is, "No, not usually."

A person who needs a few sips of water to speak publicly is feeling nervous. The person who has a knot in his or her stomach the size of a golf ball or maybe even a baseball probably has a little anxiety. The student whose heart is beating a little fast and who is perspiring ounces rather than gallons while standing to speak in front of a teacher and class, just feels the usual amount of discomfort public speaking creates in most people.

Again, using the word *disproportional* is key to understanding and reading extreme body signals as being more about regression than about present-time nervousness. Extreme body cues indicate we need to deal with and perhaps heal the wounds of the past so our body can relax, allowing us to be more effective in our present endeavors. These extreme body signals say that rage or other disproportional reactions are about to spill out.

Believing There Is No Choice

When I asked Charlotte why she didn't leave her verbally abusive husband, she said, "Because I don't have that choice." When I asked Arnold why he doesn't quit the job that offered no chance for advancement or increase in pay, he, too, replied, "I didn't have a choice."

When adults feel they have no choice, they become angry/enraged or depressed/passive, and are usually in a regressed state. It often takes someone else (who is not regressed) to offer them choices, point out options, because the regressed person can't hear them, see them, or act on them.

"You just don't understand," says Charlotte. "I have to stay with him. Besides, sometimes it's not that bad. If it were just me, maybe I could leave him. But we have children to think of, so I just don't have the option."

Arnold said, "I have too many bills to pay and a kid in college and another about to graduate from high school and go to college. I can't quit my job. I just have to grit my teeth, suck it up, and stay at a job that really sucks."

When working with people who feel and think that they really don't have a choice I first have to help them see their regression, deal with the triggers that are sending them back in time, explore their emotional memory, and hopefully facilitate a discharge and release of the pent-up energy, whether it is rage or sadness.

Once this is accomplished, then I can help them see the choices that have been right in front of them all along. Now a friend of theirs can offer suggestions, their pastor can recommend books to read. But if others' well-intended help is offered before such people come out of their regression, it all falls on deaf ears. I'm sure you've had these frustrating conversations with friends who tell you about a crisis or a problem they are having and you pull out your best advice, lovingly giving them options and choices, for them only to respond with, "You just don't understand," "No I can't do that," or "I wish it was that easy."

Not Talking Enough

Your partner, boss, or friend looks at you impatiently with baited breath, drumming his or her fingers on the kitchen table while waiting for you to talk. The silence is deafening. Forgetting that you are a forty-year-old and not a child of four, the person asks, "So what do you have to say for yourself?" Or perhaps these tried and failed words are spoken while you are lost in your history: "I don't hear anything" or "You *do* know it is your turn to talk."

THE PHYSIOLOGY AND BRAIN
CHEMISTRY OF CHOICELESSNESS

Choice is a function of the neocortex, or the new brain. Scientists tell us this portion of the human brain is roughly ten thousand years old. This new brain is capable of rational and logical thought processes. According to Antonio Damasio, author of *The Feeling of What Happens*, the neocortex permits "fine perceptions, language, and high reason. It allows us to 'think' about our choices and reason out our options." In contrast, the neocortex and the developed prefrontal lobes are basically inactive during the regressed state.

During regression, it is our reptilian, or "old brain," that is in charge. This section of the human brain is what we share with reptiles; it has been keeping humans safe for over one hundred thousand years. This brain is only capable of controlling our most basic functions—eating, excreting, and procreating—and is limited to dealing with a threat to our physical or emotional survival—real or imagined. It tells us to do one of three things—fight, flight, or freeze.

When a painful, traumatic, hurtful, or unpleasant memory is triggered, we leave the neocortex, bypass the limbic or mammal brain, and head straight to the reptilian brain. As Dr. Peter Levine states in his seminal work, *Waking the Tiger*, "For the reptile, conscious choice is not an option." He goes further to say, "The neocortex is not powerful enough to override the instinctual defense response to threat and danger."

The other option is to run away from the perceived threat to somewhere safe, like a genuine cave or the cave of our own mind, and hide until we are out of danger. If we can't do either, we go into freeze mode, or suspended animation, for the duration of the threat, such as a bad marriage or less-than-desirable work situation. In other words, when we are in this state, our choices that can be seen by others regarding our particular regressive situation cannot be seen by us until we return to the neocortex.

Temporarily mute, you search the corners of your mind for the right words that can be used to resolve the conflict before shrugging and blurting out, "I don't have anything to say," "What do you want me to say?" or "Just write it up and I'll confess and sign," or you just storm out of the room.

The words won't come. Hours later, you finally think of what you should have said and repeat the responses over and over in your head. No longer dumbfounded, you return to the logical, reasonable, rational, choice-making, word-choosing portion of the brain and then analyze what went wrong. You realize you weren't being grilled by an irate parent but just an angry spouse. Or you understand it wasn't the junior high principal that caught you smoking when you were thirteen; rather, a boss who wanted to know why the project you were working on wasn't finished.

When the right words come too late, you feel foolish, small, and certainly less powerful than you usually are. The tightening in the chest, the clenched jaw, and the grinding your teeth at night are all still there. The tension and stress of holding in what you meant to say is locked into your body, and is not set free until you get the release you long for, which may be followed by rage.

Talking yet Not Saying Anything

Cynthia and her life partner, Rokelle, came to see me for a consultation. Cynthia is a tall, blond, in her midthirties. She graduated from Brown and works for Merrill-Lynch. Rokelle is a bodybuilder who never attended college but has an IQ that is off the charts. They agreed they had serious problems

communicating and both were conflict avoidant. Cynthia admitted this readily but admitted her real frustration and rage
came during arguments or disagreements, because Rokelle
could talk circles around her. Cynthia said, "I can't make a coherent sentence when we fight. I will talk and talk and she —,"
pointing to Rokelle, "looks at me and says things like, 'what are
you trying to say?' or 'I don't understand a word you just said,'
and it is so frustrating. I don't even know what I said. I go from
an articulate, college graduate and senior account manager to
a babbling idiot who can't put two words together. What's up
with that? It doesn't make any sense." Cynthia sat back in her
chair and threw her hands up into the air. Rokelle looked at her
and smiled and then looked at me. "She's right. She's brilliant
and could be a professional public speaker, but when we argue
I can't understand a word she's saying. I joke with her and tell
her she needs to join the 12-step program called On and On
and get some help." Cynthia's face turned red as she responded,
"She's right, though I hate to admit it."

Talking without really saying anything is a signal of regression and is closely connected to feeling as if you don't have a
choice. When people are regressed, they often lose their ability
to choose the right words at the right time. Their brain is not as
connected to their tongue, in part because they are on that rapid
journey from the neocortex to the reptilian brain, where accu-
rate, articulate speech is unavailable.

Conflicts, arguments, disagreements, squabbles, or whatever
you want to call them, send many people back in time. Take

two highly intelligent adults, trigger two emotional memories, and before you know it, they both sound like teenagers trying to work out their issues.

Most people grow up never seeing conflict and confrontations expressed gracefully and resolved successfully. Instead, someone would storm out of the house in a fury. Others screamed, yelled, or dished out the silent treatment or, worse, got hit, slapped, pushed, or shoved—or indulged in those behaviors themselves. As soon as a conflict arises in the present, such people descend back to those unpleasant or painful times and use the methods they saw modeled for them so long ago. They attack or retreat from their partner/opponents/spouse/enemy, co-worker/conspirator only to discover one more time that those methods didn't work effectively back then and they still don't work today.

Thinking You Know Best

"I know my brother better than he knows himself," said Andrew during a phone consultation. Andrew is a CEO of a large sign manufacturing company in Chicago and his brother, Rodney, is his sales manager. "Rodney has always had problems ever since we were kids. I've always looked out for him. I mean, I'm the older brother. That was my job then and it's still my job today. Rodney needs to go into rehab and that's why I'm calling you to get your advice on where I should send him. He's got a huge cocaine addiction. I'm pretty certain it should be the Betty Ford people."

I listened and, once Andrew paused, I asked, "So how old is Rodney?" "Oh, my baby brother will be sixty in December."

There are several issues we could address if we were to look at Andrew's statements about his brother, but perhaps less obvious is the issue regarding Andrew's impossible ability to know what is best for another adult. There is no way we can "know" what another person needs to do or, for that matter, if the individual even has a problem. Certainly we can guess based on experience, education, training, and association with people, but we can't know for sure. Most of us aren't really sure what we, ourselves, need most of the time, much less know what others need.

Where does this insatiable need to *know* come from? More often than not, it comes from our childhood. Children know a lot more than adults give them credit for. They don't "know" in an intellectual or cognitive way. They know in their guts, their body, and, most of all their, heart. It is this "felt" knowing that allows or enhances a child's ability to survive dysfunctional families, stress, confusion, and turmoil.

In this way, children can sense that something is wrong. Daddy is not sick or tired, he's drunk; Momma doesn't really have a headache, she's depressed; Brother is not on vacation, he's been sent to jail. Bottom line, children know when something is wrong, when a lie is being told to them, and when they're hearing the truth.

When adults think they know what another adult needs to do, say, or be, it is usually because they are, themselves, regressing. They become the scared children who must know and take steps to contain what is frightening them, in order to navigate or survive what is going on. They return to their felt sense or feeling that something is wrong and then soothe and comfort themselves by convincing themselves and trying to convince others that they know much more than they do (or possibly can know). They take on a fake parental role and think they are doing the right thing for everyone involved.

Thinking they know best is a message that says to another person, "I am better, smarter, and more adult than you are." Such messages regress the hearer even further and convey a holier-than-thou, one-up, putting-down, critical, and shaming attitude toward the listener. All of these, if you recall, are forms of rage and signals that the *speaker* is regressing.

A woman called me a few days ago. "I've read all your books and listened to all your CDs and I'm absolutely certain my husband needs to come see you for counseling." I smiled and said, "I'm sorry, there's no way you can know this. Does he say he needs counseling?"

"No, of course not, but I've lived with the man for twenty-five years."

"What about you? Do you need counseling?"

"I don't have a clue," she said, as we both laughed.

During a relationships workshop a few years ago, I was having couples write down how their partners or spouses liked to be touched, what their favorite food was, and what their favorite movie or TV show was. Then they shared their answers with their partner. No one got more than 50 percent of the answers correct, but almost everyone said they *thought* they knew the right answer.

Can't Ask for Help

Young children are very often helpless and need a great deal of attention and assistance. Unfortunately, by early midadolescence, they all but have stopped asking for it. Before I go any further let's recognize that this is changing, that asking for help today is not looked down upon nearly as much as it was twenty, thirty, or forty years ago. Also we must recognize that it is better today, although many boys—and even some girls—are encouraged to never admit they need help. Growing up in the 1950s, '60s, and '70s, asking for help was a sign of weakness or inferiority. The self-made man; someone living up to Thoreau's code of self-reliance; the strong, silent John Wayne hero—although not paid much attention to today—was then many a child's idea of manhood and womanhood.

Throughout Paul's childhood, teen years, and most of his adult life, he thought that if you went to see a psychologist or psychiatrist you were "crazy," "insane," or just plain weak. Even when he was fifty, this rural Southern construction worker—who drank whiskey like water and watched football every Sunday—didn't tell his wife he was coming to see me. He'd known her since high school and had been married to her for over thirty years. When I asked him why he had to keep this a secret from her, his neck and face became flushed and he tightened his jaw, "A couple of years ago, she and I weren't getting along so well. I brought up the idea of seeing a counselor and she asked me if

---

EXERCISE

Make a list of all the things you "think" you know about someone—spouse, adult child, parent, business partner, or friend; such as, "My husband needs to go into therapy; my wife needs to call her mother and work out her issues; the woman my son is dating is not right for him." (Don't forget to have some fun here and be honest). Now find a relaxing place and sit down with the one you wrote about. Go over it with the person and listen to his or her responses.

I was gay. She said that if I was gay she didn't want anybody knowing that and that we could work out any problem we had and didn't need anyone sticking their nose in our business. I told her of course I wasn't gay and that was the end of our conversation. But the truth is I'm not sure that I love her like I should and I need someone to talk to about this. That doesn't mean I'm gay—does it? It still pisses me of that she said that or even thought of it."

As we all know, men don't ask for directions. One time, my wife and I were a half hour late getting to an out-of-town event. She said, "We're lost. Why don't we stop by that gas station and ask for directions?" I kept my eyes on the road. "Lost? I'm not lost, I'm just temporarily not sure where I am!" She burst out laughing and, after seeing what I was doing, I laughed right along with her. But I still didn't ask for directions.

Just yesterday I spoke with a man in Detroit who wanted to talk about how scared he was and how he felt disconnected from his family. He went on to say, "I own a very successful corporation, we have a beautiful home, new cars, the whole bit. But the truth is, I'm very insecure."

I said, "At the thought of sitting down and telling your wife and two teenage sons just how scared you get sometimes and how disconnected and insecure you are, what feelings or emotions surface?"

Without taking a breath he said, "Oh, I could never do that. My sons look up to me. I'm their role model and their hero. I would never want them to know this."

"So basically, you want them to think you are someone you're not and that you don't really need anyone's help or support, and you are teaching them to walk through life the way you have had to all your life—looking, acting, and sounding stronger than you really are."

"Yeah, I hate that, but I'm never going to tell them how insecure I am."

And so the cycle continues whereby people act some other way than they really feel. When they do, there are misunderstandings and miscommunication, but most of all, "acting" instead of being is perpetuated, and this very often results in anger and rage. I have said to many, "Where there are roles, there is rage." A role is both a disservice to the one playing the role and to those who watch.

The Triangle Tangle

In the words of Rod Serling, the narrator of the hugely popular 1950s television series, *The Twilight Zone*: "You are traveling through another dimension, a dimension of not only sight and sound but of mind . . . Next stop, the Twilight Zone," or perhaps the emotional Bermuda Triangle. Many a good man or woman has been emotionally lost for decades. They just disappeared into an emotional netherworld where no one talks to anyone directly, where family secrets are shared but not with everyone, where nothing is aboveboard or out in the open. This "no-man's land" is in the narrow confines of a triangle.

Everyone has heard of a "love triangle," but there is also a rage triangle. Triangulation is like emotional strangulation, in the sense that you can't speak to someone directly the words you want to or need to. The more dysfunctional a home is, the more it is filled with these triangles, and the more we see, hear, and participate in them—and perpetuate them in the present— the angrier we become. A rage triangle's main purpose is to convey uncomfortable messages to others *through* others, and often those communications break down. Very often there is also a failed attempt to also receive answers via another person.

Steven's mother tells him about his sister. Steven talks to his sister about his father. His father talks to his sister about Steven, and so on. Steven said to me, "It's been this way for over five decades and I hate it but, I don't know how to break out of it; we've done it for so long."

These triangles, whether they are constructed at home or work, become "the tangled web we weave" because, at a certain level, we are actually being deceptive through omission and we are depriving ourselves and others of the benefits adults can have by speaking directly to those we need to speak to.

The damage done by "going behind their back," or "going through the back door," or "taking the roundabout way" gets everyone involved a little or a lot angry and increases mistrust and distrust.

Ted said, "I called my ex-wife to find out how my oldest son, Bill, is doing and I asked her to ask him to call me."

"What kept you from calling him directly?" I asked.

"I feel that he dismissed me from his life years ago. He told me he didn't want to have anything to do with an alcoholic father."

"When was that?" I asked.

"About twenty years ago when I was drinking."

"Are you still drinking?"

"Oh no, I've been clean and sober for five years. But every time I think about calling him I hear those words of his in my ears like it was yesterday."

How do you demolish triangles? By making more straight lines. By going directly to the person, family, group, teacher, or boss and saying what you need to say and/or asking for what you need.

THE HEALING TRIANGLE

Not all triangles are dysfunctional. When we get to a deeper discussion of The Detour Method, it becomes clear that Ted (in the previous example) may need to go to someone outside his family circle to experience and express his feelings around having been "dismissed" before going to his son. This could take the form of talking about his feelings to a friend, therapist, sponsor, or someone else he trusts. Once he has safely released his pent-up feelings, he can drop the old baggage of his previous alcoholic behaviors and meet his son man-to-man in the present.

The unhealthy, inefficient triangle is a dysfunctional detour and never brings the taker or maker of the triangle to the heart of the matter and certainly not to the heart of someone he or she cares about, and meanwhile the person in the third corner feels put-upon or increases the disconnect by picking and choosing or warping what is being communicated through him or her. Everyone becomes the victim of the closed triangle system and that is why there is so much rage among all involved.

Ted's son called me for a session after his mother called him for her ex-husband and said, "My mother said that Dad has been in counseling with you and that he seems to have changed . . . " We talked for about twenty minutes before he finally said, "I'm so mad at my dad. Why doesn't he have the balls to call me himself if he wants to know how I am or who I am? He didn't care about knowing me when I was a kid and it seems like he hasn't changed at all. When I get off the phone with you, I'm going to call him and give him a piece of my mind."

I said, "You can do that, but may I suggest you and I work on how you have come to be so passive in your relationships specifically and in your life in general, and how you have waited for things and people to be different than they are. Then we will take this thing called The Detour Method first, so you can get to your feelings about him from twenty years ago. Understanding and working with your passivity is an important step in the process."

Chapter 4

Passivity: The Hidden Producer of Rage

For decades, the following forms of rage and expressions of regression have been focused on by dozens of writers in the field of anger management and by numerous psychologists:

- Passive/Aggressive
- Aggressive
- Violent
- Abusive

But a key form of rage that until now has not been identified is what I call passive rage. Passive rage, or passivity, is the least understood because it is the most overlooked aspect of human behavior and how it impacts on all kinds of relationships, almost always very negatively.

Passivity is not timidity, shyness, laziness, or apathy; much has been written on all these behaviors. Passivity is an unconscious compulsion to replay the feelings and memories we've stored in our brain and body since childhood, while avoiding engaging with the present. What we've been discussing and illustrating up to this point in *The Anger Solution* is mostly the dysfunctional and unhealthy verbal and emotional forms rage and regression can take.

When asked, "Who are you the angriest at in your past or present life?" nine of out ten people say "at me" right off the bat.

The person who answers this way is usually suffering from either mild or extreme passivity. Passivity then is an act of rage (not anger) against the self. Passivity is a negation of ourselves, our dreams, our goals, and our successes in all of areas of life. Passivity is personal, sometimes permanent and terminal, absenteeism. We're not *there* for ourselves because we are so *angry* or *raging* at ourselves. At that point, passivity is self-aggression in its worst form. This self-aggression comes in many different disguises ranging from low self-worth to self-hatred. Passive people are full of self-doubt, self-condemnation, and criticize everything they say, do, and think, especially when they perceive they have failed at something or not achieved their or someone else's goals or standards.

Unlike the previous examples given in the earlier chapters, passivity is an offense of omission rather than of commission. For example, shaming is—at even some unhealthy level—engaging with another person. But passive people never truly engage with another person because they have discarded themselves (usually very early on in life).

In an early work of mine, *The Flying Boy Book II*, I say, "Adults can't be abandoned." When I say this at workshops or

enmeshed with them and unable to model secure boundaries. They produce children who are unable to separate and who resort to passivity as a way to cope. These often well-intentioned parents overprotect, push, and prod their children to be winners, the best, a success, or superachievers, but they are actually provoking many children into adult passivity.

Passive people very often enter a perpetual state of waiting. They wait for the "love object" (to use neo-Freudian term) to return but never mourn or become angry about their loss. The passive person waits in vain for the parent they are less bonded to—or in bondage to—to set them free, so they will no longer live their life vicariously through that person anymore.

Daniel is a client who picks the same love interest over and over again. "It's like I can't break out of picking women who leave me for another man, another city, or another job. It's like I'm picking women who are much more like my dad who left me and mom when I was twelve. He had a whole different family whom he paid a great deal of attention to and only sent us the occasional birthday or Christmas card with a check stuck in."

Linda said, "My mother was always on top of me. It's like I couldn't take a breath without her. I don't think I have any childhood memories that don't also include my mother's being right there. I swore I'd never be that mother to any of my three children. We were in family therapy a couple of years ago and the two oldest boys, one is twelve and the other is fifteen, said, 'Mom, you were never there for us. Where were you?' I said I just wanted to give you boys the space I never had, to grow and be your own person."

Two Types of Adult Passivity
Obviously Passive

These individuals' shoulders are bowed toward the ground. They carry the weight of the world. Their chest is tight and constricted and breathing is shallow. They lack self-confidence, have minimal sense of mastery over danger, and feel destiny and fate control them. This creates a great deal of nervousness, anger, and anxiety. They appear to be worried about all the things that may befall them. When they are not worried, their mind looks more like stagnant water because they are often bored and uninterested in much of anything. Their speech is slow and they speak in clichés, using little or no original, creative language: "Cool," "Wow," "Terrific," "Great," "Whatever," "Fine," "It's all good," "It is what it is," and so on. They have poor or little memory. Crucial events are minimized. They make little or no distinctions between peak and mundane experiences.

The Disguised Passive Person

These people keep their body taut and tense; they have locked knees and their speech is accelerated to a rapidfire pace. They are always hyperbusy and overestimate their talents and capabilities. They feel superior to those around them because they think they are more endowed creatively, spiritually, intellectually, financially, and so on.

Dr. Fried, in her academic text *Active/Passive*, points out that the obviously passive and the disguised passive types display one or more of the following passive styles when they were infants and early in their childhood.

Three Types of Passivity in Children
Barrier Passivity

Barrier passivity is the result of children sending out disregarded signals that they are in discomfort. They scream, fret, and then nothing happens because so many cries for help are unanswered. So they finally find themselves behind a kind of emotional barricade. They barricade their needs behind immobility and silence. This is often the child who says, "Look, Momma, I'm dead." They play dead and at some level it's because that's how they feel. Can you see the anger/rage that results?

Plea Passivity

If a parent enjoys too much closeness, children may crave even more attention and intervention on their behalf. Rather than nurturing and fostering separation, the children get stuck in a high, unhealthy level of dependency, which turns the adult into an extremely dependent personality with a "Give me," "Do it for me," or "I'm entitled" stance in life. These people have an insatiable need for indulgence that will dramatically increase the likelihood they will become an addict or alcoholic, one of the truest symptoms of passivity there is.

Alibi Passivity

Dr. Fried goes on to point out this is a very common form of passivity that children, and that teenagers especially slip into. "My legs are too short to play basketball. If I had longer legs, I'd play and I'm sure I'd be great at it." "If I had received a better education, then I could have gotten into that Ivy League university."

"No one in my family is good with math." When they become adults, the rhetoric is similar: "I was raised on the wrong side of the tracks," "I don't have the time," "Maybe I'll follow my dream when the kids are out of school," "All the good ones are taken." Alibi passivity puts the blame on environment or circumstances, clothing a self-imposed lack of choice and possibilities.

How to Identify Passivity in Yourself

One of the main markers of passive people is that they are seldom, if ever, concerned about their passivity but will quickly become enraged or outraged when they see it in others.

Bill, who suffers with his own passivity issues, spent hours in a two-day intensive with me last year, raging at his father for being so passive with his mother when he was a boy. "He never stood up to her, his boss, or anyone for that matter. He was the stereotypical 'doormat.' When my mother or even my grandparents criticized him harshly, he just stood there and took it. I was embarrassed for him."

Another indicator of individuals' being plagued by passivity is their being embarrassed by the behaviors, actions, and words of another. "I need you to be or not be a certain way because it reflects well or poorly on me. I do as well or badly as you do," is the passive person's credo.

Passive people focus on the character flaws of others through criticism or care-taking, leaving little or no time for them to look inward at their own issues, wounds, pain, or abandonment issues. Another trick passive people play on themselves is, "Look how hard I am trying to help my wife, son, daughter, parent, and business partner get help for their problems and how much I am always there for them. How can anyone see me as passive?" or "Look at how hard I work at my job, or what a success I am. I work eighty hours a week. How can anyone say I'm passive?" A person or family who loves someone who works this much is almost always angry, resentful, and depressed.

Depression can stem from a chemical problem such as a serotonin deficiency, hormone disorder, or other illness. But current research indicates that less than 10 percent of clinical depression is thought to have a chemical basis. The majority of depression is triggered by nonbiochemical situations such as stress, anxiety, insomnia, and emotional regression (just to name a few).

I have worked with many men and women who are plagued with nonbiochemical depression caused by their passivity. This depression is brought about because the regressed, passive people repress feelings, emotions, needs, wants, words, actions, and behaviors on a daily basis. To hold these inside requires a tremendous amount of available energy. At the end of a regular, repressed day, these individuals are not feeling angry, frustrated, or disappointed; they are exhausted, so they withdraw even further into their shell, hanging an invisible Do Not Disturb sign on their back.

Sandy remembers his father's working twelve to sixteen hours a day, and when he finally did come home, "He went straight to the fridge and pulled out a six-pack, sat down in his favorite chair—aptly named La-Z-Boy—read the paper, turned on the television, and went to sleep. It was like he was there but not really." His father was, like many men and women, depressed to the point of passivity. Such people are there but not really involved, engaged, or taking an active role in their own lives or the lives of their loved ones.

It is important to note that, more often than not, nonbio-chemical depression can be treated through emotional release work involving discharge and catharsis. This may take several active sessions, but I have seen positive results literally thousands of times over the last two decades of my career of facilitating emotional-release work and teaching people how to do so themselves.

Signs of Problems with Passivity

The following signs may indicate that a person is passive:

- Extreme loneliness
- Feeling cut off
- Trouble making friends
- Emotional unavailability
- Feeling victimized
- Powerlessness

Extreme Loneliness

Having worked with men over the years, I know this is especially true for men who tend to keep a small number of intimate friendships even when they're not passive. When asked how many men can you comfortably bare your soul to, most men respond: none. Or as Darryl said the other day at a workshop in New York, "I got this one guy who lives in Seattle that I grew up with and we try to stay in touch every now and then, and I have a few golfing and drinking buddies, but I'd never tell them anything *really* personal."

When it comes time to talk about deep personal issues, passivity takes its toll. In the case of Marjorie, who says, "I was never really close friends with other women and because my husband is so jealous, I don't really have any male friends like I did when I was in high school and college. I mostly tell him everything and what I can't tell him, I usually just keep it to myself. I guess I take a little too much to him sometimes and want him to comfort me when I'm regressed. Sometimes this seems to make him very angry and then I get a little enraged when he doesn't pay the kind of attention to me that I sometimes crave."

Feeling Cut Off

Passive people tend to isolate themselves and feel cut off, viewing themselves as constant outsiders. Instead of looking at their passivity, they rage or remain silent and blame those around them for not being more available.

Trouble Making Friends

Passive people not only have trouble making friends, many are perplexed and frustrated when they find themselves not as well equipped as they would like to be to give or receive mature love. The nonpassive person actively engages with and displays an interest in and love toward others. They can take positive

hen someone wants to deliver them to their
...e passive person tends to focus on how well or
poorly they perceive they are loved, and regard such overtures
with suspicion—if they pick up on them at all.

Emotional Unavailability

Passive people hear: "Why don't you open up?" or "When are
you going to let me in?" The answers such individuals usually
give if they get active enough to even respond to such a question are: "I'm not sure what you mean" or "I don't know how,"
but the most truthful answer would be, "Never, unless I can
come out of my passivity."

Feeling Victimized

Sometimes passive people feel the world is against them and
that's why they fail in relationships and other endeavors. Because these people show so little interest in healing their passivity issues, therapists often become very annoyed and
frustrated with such clients. Edretta Fried, in her book *Ac-
tive/Passive*, says, "The passive patient is prematurely discharged
largely because of dormant resentment he creates in others."

Powerlessness

Passive people will often feel as if they are always being "done
to," not like they are doing. They experience the world and
other people as having most of the control over their lives,
whereas they have little or none. They say things like, "That's
the way the cookie crumbles," "I guess it wasn't meant to be,"

"It wasn't in the cards," and "I guess I'm just unlucky." They feel deprived, denied, missing out, ignored, gypped, ripped off, ineffectual, and unessential. Their motto at work or home is, "Say nothing, do nothing, feel nothing," "Grit your teeth and bear it," or "Don't rock the boat," or as T. S. Eliot says in *The Love Song of J. Alfred Prufrock*, "Do I dare disturb the universe." Erich Fromm said, "A passive person is . . . an eternal suckling babe . . . he simply waits, with open mouth . . . "

Fran said she is scared that she and her husband were going to lose the big, expensive McMansion they bought after he got promoted, and she has harbored a great deal of resentment because she was absolutely opposed to getting it. Now he is about to be laid off. "Have you told him about your resentment and fears?" I asked.

"No. I don't want to rock the boat. We haven't had an argument in several weeks."

Passivity and Rage

All of these factors combine to make passive people full of rage. Every time they feel acted upon, not loved enough, or disconnected from themselves and others, their rage intensifies and deepens and very often turns into negative grandiosity and pseudoaggression.

Passive individuals harbor intense fantasies to become the dominant one who can punish or oppress all those around them. Some of the most negative, grandiose people actually use their out-of-balance energies to become pseudopowerful.

It may take the form of the father who rules his kingdom/home with an iron will or fist, or a despot or demigod who rules a country with tyranny. Such people cover up their passivity with rage.

Fear of the Word *Passivity*

Passivity is obvious in many women, especially those born in the early and mid-twentieth century. The mothers of many baby boomers were indoctrinated into their passive roles. They were supposed to be the women who suffer quietly in the kitchen or the bedroom and never try to gain access to the boardroom or public eye because that would be seen as being too aggressive and unladylike. Thanks to the women's movement in the 1960s and '70s, now they can suffer in the boardroom or on the battlefield and be as aggressive, pseudoaggressive, or passive/aggressive as men were trained and encouraged to be. However, with all the bad and good things that came with all of this, they still are encouraged to not get too angry or too assertive. But progress has been made.

The Masculine Protest

Unfortunately, progress has been very slow with the smaller, lesser-known men's movement of the 1980s and early 1990s. We did make some headway, or I should say *heartway*, regarding a form of passivity in men that has had almost nothing written on it, what Freud and others have called "the masculine protest."

For centuries, men have been told (and many have been convinced) that *passive* equals *feminine*. Because our modern culture has oppressed women and seen them as the "fairer" or "weaker" sex (that is changing in Generations X and Y, but is still present), femininity was something to be feared as a negative characteristic to be avoided at all costs. In their attempt to never be seen as feminine, many men turn their back on anything that smacks of femininity or homosexuality—especially emotions. This explains in part why many men's emotional intelligence is so stunted. Rather than being seen as passive, weak, or feminine/effeminate, many men become hypermacho, hyperactive, aggressive, and career/money driven, and thus are never accused of passivity or femininity.

In the play *Twelve Angry Men*, juror number ten says, "What do you want us to do, sit here all night and discuss your feelings?" with absolute disdain in his tone of voice. If men have little or no access to their emotions and confident women are still called *bitches* or worse if they show too much assertiveness or anger, then rage will be the result and passivity will be the wall we hide behind, be we male or female.

Ken said to me during a phone consultation, "I stay busy all the time. Even when I get ready to go jogging to relax and unwind, I change clothes in the car at stop signs and red lights. I'm running all the time. Yesterday I woke up crying when I remembered a dream about my ex-girlfriend. I know this sounds silly, but I thought, 'What if I'm gay?' That would explain why I'm forty-six and never married. If I spent anytime examining the answer to this question, all I could think of was all the women I could have dated, which would prove I'm not gay or passive. So I jumped out of bed and I didn't stop working at my office until twelve that night."

Countless anonymous sexual encounters can be a smoke-screen for not wanting to appear vulnerable or deal with one's passivity, or feelings of being inferior or appearing too feminine. These are the kinds of feelings men have been projecting onto women for a long time, resulting in rage on the part of both sexes.

The anger and rage being expected to act "feminine" creates in women is to be expected and no longer needs to be denied for more adult behavior to result. But this rejection of things associated with "the feminine" remains one of men's greatest regressions. Men, too, must face the unhealthy education and indoctrination they received as boys, regarding the feminine. For compassion to replace fear of castration and of being labeled gay, sissy, pansy, and other juvenile tags, with the regard, respect, and appreciation of the feminine in men—in whatever form it is found—must be modeled by adult men and women for our children's sake, if not our own.

The passive man, or as Dr. Russell Davis points out in his book *Freud's Concept of Passivity*, the man who fears passivity because it has come to be associated with feminine traits, must go back into his history as soon as possible. Then he will feel the unexpressed feelings he had when someone would in some way question his masculinity.

Robert Bly and I spoke at a men's gathering last year in the mountains of Alabama, which my wife, Susan, and I call home. At the gathering, Brad told a story about when he was six years old. "One night, I went into the living room where my dad was watching a ball game and drinking with some guys who worked for him. I leaned over and tried to kiss him good night. He turned to me with whiskey on his breath, then looked at his drinking buddies and said, 'Now, aren't you the little girl? You don't ever kiss a man, I don't care who it is.' If that didn't take something out of me, the next statements tore a hole in my soul. 'Would you fellas look at my little girl here? Isn't she sweet? What do you think about a boy still wanting to kiss his father, a big boy like him? From now on, you shake hands and never, ever let me see you kiss a man again, or I'll break you into little pieces. Now get to bed, you little sissy.' There was something gone in me after that. I never trusted him again, or other men; and I have always questioned my sexuality, not to mention my masculinity."

Brad's emotional release and discharge of his intense anger, rage, and grief was so powerful that afternoon that it sent shivers down the spine of many of the men at the conference who had experienced various kinds of rejection of the gentler parts of themselves.

Living Vicariously

This leads to the final indicator of passivity both in the men and women. The passive person tends to be compelled or addicted to experiencing vicariously the world and the creativity that animates the world and makes it interesting. My generation had three TV stations and movies that allowed for some passive vicarious experiences. The youth and adults today have five hundred stations, DVDs, the Internet, video games, virtual sex, and many other artificial realities that are becoming more and more sophisticated and prevalent each day.

By saying we live vicariously, I mean we live by artificially, *acquiring* rather than *accessing* the genuine adventurer, storyteller, magician, lover, feminine, or masculine inside us. Accessing requires an active imagination and active engagement of our own talents, ideas, and facets of ourselves. Electronics and media immerse us in a virtual world—*virtual* meaning "simulated," as opposed to "real"—that further induces us into a passive coma, wherein we are acted upon instead of acting on the world and the people around us, which then further deepens the regression and rage in us as a culture and society. Americans are quickly becoming one of the most passive people playing on the world stage.

Solutions and Cures for Passivity

The bottom line is: Passivity is the compulsion to try to get what we are desperately longing for, while doing all the wrong things or nothing to get it. (Note: This should not be confused with patience, which is knowing something worth waiting for is just around the corner—and taking appropriate steps to get closer to it.) The passive person waits and waits. Passive waiting is about letting hope die by withdrawing and not taking effective action. This waiting has to stop.

Charlie is the best example of passive waiting I've worked with this year. "What do you want and need regarding your intimate life with Charlotte [his wife]?" I asked. Without a moment's hesitation he replied, "I want her to touch me more often, hold my hand, stroke my face, and make love a lot more than we do."

"How is that going?"

"Terrible. We haven't made love in over a year. I can't remember the last time we even held hands and we only give each other little pecks on the cheek now and then. I have tried. Just before coming to see you is a good example of what I mean. She watches hours of television every night. She stretches out on the couch and sometimes falls asleep and doesn't even come to bed. So for the hundredth time I went in the living room and got in front of the idiot box and said, 'Don't you think you've watched enough television for one night? I mean, there's nothing but crap on anyway. Wouldn't you rather do something more intellectually stimulating or maybe say have sex since we haven't touched each other in I don't know how long?'"

"How did that work for you?"

"Not too well. She just stared at me for a few moments until I moved and she went back to watching whatever piece of crap that was on."

"So in other words, you shamed her, demeaned her, denigrated her intelligence, blamed her, and preached the gospel according to you?" I said with a touch of humor in my tone, aware that I was channeling the often verbally abusive TV psychologists and judges who do this regularly to their guests. And then I added, "And you wonder why she didn't respond more favorably? Perhaps her television watching is her way of expressing some passive rage. May I make a suggestion?"

"Sure, that's what I'm here for is to figure out how to make my marriage work better."

"First, let's work on your passivity in your marriage instead of the marriage itself." Before I could go further, he jumped in.

"How can you say I'm passive? I'm here, aren't I? I've been going to counselors, couple's therapists, workshops, and read dozens of books including yours. How can you say I'm passive?"

"Have you ever gone into the living room while your wife is lying on the couch watching TV, picked up her legs and slid on the couch next to her, then placed her legs on your lap and started stroking or massaging her feet while you ask, 'So what are we watching tonight?'" I asked.

Charlie looked a little dumbfounded before saying, "No, I have never even thought of it. It sounds so simple. I can see me doing that but I never would have thought to do so. I wonder why," he said very seriously.

It was because of passivity and his fears of rejection, abandonment, and intimacy.

By the way, he tried my suggestion the very next week. "We got up off the couch ten minutes after doing what you suggested. She looked at me and said, 'Who are you?' Before I could answer she laughed and said, 'Never mind, I like this,' and we got up and got in bed and made love for the first time in a year."

Identifying the areas of our life where we are passive is the first part of the solution to passivity and to the regression and rage it sometimes hides.

In her book *Active/Passive*, Dr. Edrita Fried lists her solutions to passivity and the process of becoming more actively engaged in life. I've adapted her suggestions, adding some of my own words:

- Using problem-focused, inventive thinking rather than routine thinking
- Expressing yourself in freshly coined, selectively chosen language instead of generic, meaningless phrases and clichés
- Making excursions into new sections of your hometown or even other cities
- Daring a certain, safe measure of self-exposure
- Developing and refining mental skills, such as learning a new language or music lessons
- Expanding and increasing your range of emotions
- Using self-made resources rather than borrowed or vicarious resources
- Developing a richer inner life
- Not exaggerating shortcomings, in favor of increasing self-validation of strengths
- Giving up "victim language," such as, "He keeps ignoring my boundaries"
- Grieving the losses passivity has plagued your life with over the years
- Creating a community of support
- Finding the balance between personal and professional life
- Pursuing ongoing anger work

One of the main reasons for putting this material on passivity in an anger book is because all the writers of academic texts agree that one of the main ways to treat passivity is anger work. In *Active/Passive,* Dr. Fried says that anger work offers "escape routes from inertia to activeness." She goes on to say that the expression of anger and rage leads to self-understanding and insight.

By now you should know what your own triggers and issues are around anger, rage, and regression; you've also learned how to spot triggers and passivity in others. What you'll learn next is an indispensable tool to help improve all your relationships. It's called The Detour Method, and learning how to use it will change your life and that of others around you forever.

Chapter 5

The Detour Method:
The Only Tool You Need

The Detour Method™ is a unique approach to decreasing conflict and confrontation and increases the ability to communicate clearly with those you love, live with, work with, or interact with. The Detour Method, known as TDM, can reduce and even eliminate a great deal of time-consuming energy-draining frustration, irritation, and miscommunication.

As mentioned in the chapters on anger and rage, sometimes anger (and always rage) is about something in the past that is triggered in the present. TDM helps you access that past safely so you can deal with it and move on with your life in the present. Think of TDM this way: You are driving mad straight to the home of the person who triggered your disproportional reaction. But this time, instead of going directly, you decide to take a detour and go down the slower, less dangerous country road where you pay more attention to your emotional state, give yourself some time, and pull the pieces of your fragmented thoughts and emotions together. By the time you get to where you were going after you got off the unlimited-speed Autobahn emotional highway and took the more scenic route, you are ready to see the person in the present, not as someone from your past, and you are ready to speak your feelings clearly, confidently, and appropriately.

TDM can be done alone or with a facilitator. It involves honesty and active thinking and also pulls you out of passivity, all at the same time. Anyone can do it or help someone else do it. Simply put, TDM gives you a healthy choice: a detour from the usual road you take with your anger. It is a different way to deal with your anger or rage so that it is expressed in an appropriate way with the appropriate people. The result can be anything from its being extremely cathartic to your feeling mildly relieved and released. TDM is healing, positive, and life-changing. Once you learn it, you can incorporate it into all your relationships, whether at home or at work.

Whether we are aware of it or not, our past keeps popping up and blowing things out of proportion. If a person's reaction to something someone said or didn't say, or did or didn't do, is disproportional, then TDM is to be engaged to help get to a proportional response.

Back in the late 1960s and '70s, communication took a giant leap. Pop psychologists revealed that stoicism, denial, and apathy were not healthy for relationships. In previous decades, people who didn't talk, didn't feel, and didn't confront ruled and ravaged relationships. Now they were replaced by ranting, railing, and raging people who "called people on their shit," or "told it like it is," "didn't hold back," and "spoke their mind," no matter who was hurt in the process.

Men and women were going straight to each other and unloading, dumping, and verbally bludgeoning each other all in the name of "not holding anything back." In the aftermath of such sharing, hearts and souls were seared by the heat of the unburdeners' rage. People's self-esteem slithered out of the room so low they didn't need to open doors, it just slid out underneath. This direct approach disturbed me and I just intuitively felt there had to be a better way. That way took a few more years to create.

Ultimately, using The Detour Method and working with regression can positively impact all our relationships.

Venting has gotten a terrible reputation; we all tend to do it rather unconsciously, and when we do, we tend to vent to the wrong person, not separating people and events in the past from those in our present. The Detour Method, based on the human need to vent occasionally, employs "Conscious Venting" that encourages those who need to let off steam to dialogue with themselves or choose people who will listen without judgment. This form of venting is cathartic, nonviolent, and even energizing. Most of all, it helps people stop erasing those they love, care about, or work with and see them for who they are in the present moment. One thing I've learned over the years is that people hate it when they don't feel really seen. This lack of validation tends to send them into emotional regression by triggering their emotional memories, sending them back to the many times in the past when they didn't feel seen or heard. So what may start out as one speaker being stuck in the past becomes two when the vent sends the listener into the past as well. The Detour Method prevents this from happening.

How TDM Identifies and Works with the Causes of Regression

As you discovered in the previous chapters, the causes of emotional regression are many and vary from person to person. What triggers an emotional memory for you might never regress your spouse, parent, or business partner. Likewise, what causes other people to regress wouldn't bother you on your worst day. This is why such responses by a nonregressed person as, "Why are you letting that bother you so much?" or "Don't take it personally," or "Why are you letting _____ get to you so much?" are truly some of the most useless, irritating, and regressive phrases in communication.

The Detour Method recognizes that everyone's history is unique. While many of us share aspects, experiences, circumstances, and situations, no two people—including identical twins—are exactly the same. This requires that anyone working with TDM suspend all prior judgments of themselves or (if they are facilitating) of the regressed person, remembering that feeling judged or not really heard is a major trigger for regression.

The main objectives of The Detour Method are to separate rage from anger, change emotional chaos into manageable issues, move from imagined fear and fantasy into reality, and come out of the past and into the present. These functions minimize the damage we can do while in a regressed state. Another important purpose of TDM is to begin to consciously explore our emotional memories and to unload some of the painful baggage most of us carry into many of our relationships, by choosing the right time, place, objective, and person to work with us on our recurring anger and rage issues.

These unique functions are effective in direct proportion to our ability to identify our physical, mental, and emotional cues and signals that regression is taking place. When regression begins, there is a sense that we—or our particular corner of the world—is fragmenting; or, as some say, "coming apart at the seams." TDM brings a sense of structure and organization to our real or imagined chaos. The elegant, simplicity of the program puts the pieces back together and restores order and allows us to regain some control over volatile emotions.

Another way to think about TDM is as a vehicle that transports us from the fight, flight, or freeze portion of the reptilian brain back to our more logical, reasonable neocortex. By doing this, we reduce or perhaps eliminate our sense of being in danger or being emotionally or physically injured. TDM shrinks our exaggerated emotions relating to our past to a size proportional to the present situation.

TDM doesn't negate anger, sadness, fear, or frustration. Instead it encourages us to feel all our emotions unchecked and uncensored by ourselves or with a safe, objective person. When we employ TDM as a means to work through and come to terms with our past issues, our tendency to edit or filter flowing feelings, words, images, and memories decreases dramatically. Only after we openly express our feelings can we access and deal with the initial or core issues that may have been hurting us for decades.

The Detour Method takes into consideration the preconditions for regression. It also works with the early warning signs (see page 61) that help us catch ourselves before unconsciously and unceremoniously descending into our past.

The Six Questions in TDM Process

One of the most important aspects of TDM is that it is very easy to learn and extremely easy to use and does not require a degree in psychology. It truly is the most self-help program available. It employs six structural—yet flexible—questions that will help bring you out of your regression, reducing rage and exploring justifiable and proportional anger, sadness, fear, or hurt. These six questions potentially incorporate all five elements that bring people out of their past, out of their reptilian brain, and back into the present and the rational, logical, and reasonable portion of the brain.

There are three ways to use these six questions:

- By yourself
- With a facilitator (your working with a facilitator)
- As a facilitator (your being the facilitator working with a regressed person)

Who to Take the Detour With

If you opt not to take the Detour by yourself, the best people to do it with (always working one on one) are those who have good boundaries and limits. Here is how to determine their suitability as facilitators.

There are several types of people in this world—unsafe, kind of safe, safe, and very safe. Make your own list:

Unsafe	Kind of Safe	Safe	Very Safe
Abusive boss	Brother	Best friend	Therapist
Ex-spouse	Sister	Mother	Sponsor

Those in the "safe" and "very safe" categories are the optimal choices for people to take your regression and rage to. Why? Because these people have proven over time to really be there for you "come hell or high water," "through thick and thin," or "in good times and bad times"; they have earned your trust through firsthand experience. The safe and very safe will not judge you, shame you, or dismiss you. They accept all the different and complex parts of you, from the positive light to the gray areas to the dark and shadowy parts you may wish to hide from others but over time you've let them see.

The safe/very safe people you choose to help take you into your recent or distant past probably have become, either with you or others, familiar travelers into their respective history, consciously using TDM or some other appropriate vehicle into their own wounds, traumas, and pain. They "practice what they preach" and "walk the talk," themselves. This is one of the reasons why they can be such good, empathic listeners and askers of questions.

People you choose to facilitate TDM do not need to be professionally trained therapists or counselors, although they may be. Early on in my work with regression and TDM, we found that sometimes construction workers, clerks, and CEOs can be effective facilitators of TDM. Truth is, any emotional healthy person can be a great facilitator. Lay people, or whatever you call the average Joe, do not carry the sometimes cumbersome baggage that graduate school or medical school heaps on the backs of caring, compassionate men and women in the health-care industry. However, literally hundreds of therapists and clinicians have put such bias aside to have been trained thoroughly in TDM's approach to anger, rage, and regression, so being a professional need not in of itself rule out their suitability as facilitators.

Who Not to Take the Detour With

One of the most important factors in choosing who to do TDM with is: Your facilitator should *not* be the person who triggered your regression in the first place. Yet this is almost always the one you may seek instinctively to go to, to hope or demand he or she will say or do the "right" thing that will bring you back into the present. This person usually can't be a good facilitator because he or she may also be regressed; but even if this is not the case, such a person almost certainly cannot remain objective.

Safe people are not, themselves, in a serious regressed state about other issues that clouds or limits their ability at the time to give you good clear, attention. The more safe people you have in your inner circle or support system, the more you have to choose from if one or two can't, for any reason, effectively facilitate your Detour.

Another important factor: Make sure the person who may normally be safe or very safe is not in any way impaired by drugs or alcohol, and if he or she is, do not hesitate to suspend the Detour process.

Traits of a Great Facilitator

Potential facilitators may need to educate themselves about TDM first, but as long as they're willing to open their heart and mind and have the positive traits mentioned in this section, they'll work.

The best person to choose to take a Detour with is one who does not need to "rescue" "save," "fix," "counsel," or give feedback unless it is asked for. A Detour facilitator does not urge the regressed person to go "deeper" or "do anger work." Those needing to do the above are more often than not individuals who would rather heal your painful past than deal with their own. Someone else's traumatic or painful past can be just the diversion such a person is seeking, instead of taking his or her own journey into parts of a personal history with which the individual has been playing hide-and-seek for a long time. It also deepens the passivity of such a person.

The best facilitator of TDM will not judge, diagnose, or label the person taking the Detour, and will not offer a prognosis or chart that an individual's progress or lack thereof. The facilitator will not have an agenda, thereby letting the regressed person go where he or she needs to in his or her history—to feel what has to be felt, say what has to be said, and discharge emotions in whatever way works for the person in need of release. A good facilitator *will not need to shut the person down* out of fear or anxiety, because this listener's empathetic abilities are so great, such facilitators' having been to emotionally intense places themselves.

The facilitator becomes attuned and in sync with the person taking the Detour, to go instinctively where the one who is being facilitated goes. A good facilitator mirrors the person's body posture and breathing, and makes as much eye contact as possible.

A great Detour facilitator will monitor his or her own body very closely to make sure he or she is present and attentive. The facilitator will know if his or her own emotional memories are getting triggered by what the regressed person is saying, not saying, or doing or not doing, and if this does become the case, the facilitator will be honest, to the point if necessary, and gently interrupt the regressed person's process rather than faking attention, empathy, and contact. This is because the brilliant facilitator is a practitioner of compassionate assertiveness, to which a whole chapter will be devoted later in this book, and will have taken care of any tendencies to be codependent with the people being facilitated.

A Note on Codependency and TDM

I'm sure most reading this are familiar with the terms *codependency* and *codependent*, so I will not spend much time with these here, except only as the words relate to regression, rage, and anger. Over twenty-years ago as an early writer on the subject of codependency, I tried very hard to make this slippery recovery term more approachable and applicable to the general public. Some of this work is presented in *The Flying Boy II*. It is there that I say, "Codependency is an unfair and uneven exchange of energy, time, and concern."

Untreated codependent facilitators of TDM — or many professional therapists, for that matter — will exert more energy into another's healing process than they put into their own. They will also get less energy returned to them during a Detour with a regressed person. This is true of time and concern, as well. The best facilitators of TDM will actually be energized by extending their time and concerns to the regressed person if and only if they are putting their own well-being first. In other words, if a TDM facilitator has had an exhausting week at work and can't say no to a person who is regressed and needing a detour, the facilitator will walk — or crawl — away after a completed detour more exhausted than when or she began.

This brings me to the second explanation I developed regarding a codependent person's thinking and feeling process that directly impacts TDM's process and the regressed person taking it. The codependent is one who "is so afraid to tell you what he really thinks, really feels, and really needs for *fear* of what you *might* feel or think about what they are saying."(*The Flying Boy II*)

This fear of what someone might feel or think is a regressive tendency. It will not only compromise and even be detrimental to the detour process, it is a plague that destroys relationships of all kinds.

So, ideally, TDM facilitators take good care of themselves and don't "try" to help others at their own expense. Now, I realize you may have grown up like I did, believing people who put themselves first are "selfish." But you will find more rage and sadness in those who *don't* exercise good, self-care, because they:

- Can't say no
- Are extremely exhausted
- Are resentful
- Are depressed
- Are depleted

Codependents break their value system constantly, resulting in guilt and low self-esteem and thus increasing their tolerance for unacceptable behavior, because they give another person or process power to determine the course of their life, their moods, and their feelings. They often feel trapped and that they don't have the power to choose their own destiny, and all of this makes them very angry. If you, yourself, are feeling any of these emotions, do not attempt to be a Detour facilitator for another person, as it may only prove detrimental to you both. It might be most helpful to perform TDM privately, with yourself, to better understand your feelings.

Once you decide whether to take the Detour on your own or with a facilitator, it is time to move ahead to its six essential questions, which you will ask yourself, be asked by your facilitator, or ask the person for whom you are serving as facilitator. A facilitator should reassure the individual at the outset that he or she may speak freely and allow the person to respond to the stated questions without additional probing or analysis on the facilitator's part.

The Six Questions

1. **What is happening or going on and how am I feeling?** Answer this question as truthfully and nonjudgmentally as possible, without analyzing or intellectualizing what you are going through. Don't try to figure out anything right now, just state what the situation is and how it makes you feel. Don't edit or censor yourself and your feelings. Let them flow.

2. **Does what has just happened or is happening remind you of anyone or anything from your past?** This question often elicits a knee-jerk response, "No," or "I can't remember," or "Not that I can think of," or even a resistant, "Can't it just be about right now, in the present?" When I hear this response, I say, "Perhaps, but again let's look at the signs" (such as disproportional reactions, raging, or extreme chaos).

Sandy's husband shames her when she's sick. "I feel like he's not seeing or talking to me but to his mother, because she really was sick a lot and it was his job as a kid to take care of her. I bet I've said a hundred times, 'I'm just not feeling well today and this will pass. I'm not your mother,'" she said during part of a consultation where we were doing TDM.

When Burt was a teenager and he and his mother got into a serious fight, his mother would literally lock him in a bedroom and not let him out until he apologized to her even if she was wrong. "Now, every time my wife, Patti, and I get into a really bad fight, the first thing I think is, 'I got to get out of here right now.'" So he regularly employs the "distancer" form of rage because, as he told me, "No one will ever lock me up again, I know that's insane but that's just how I feel when we're arguing."

The more conscious closure people achieve in their life, the less likely regression and rage will occur. Like a physical wound on your body, that emotional wound needs to be closed. The heart and brain and probably the soul as well benefit from the sewing together of the past, prevent its bleeding into the present.

Rob is one of those men who spend lots of time and energy trying to be one of the healthiest people I've ever worked with. This fifty-two-year-old CEO of a chain of retail clothing stores was driving everyone crazy with his compulsive need for employees, family members, friends, and acquaintances to be punctual, to arrive at the time that was agreed upon. "I don't understand why people can't organize their lives and be somewhere when they say they will. I don't think I've ever been late for anything. Half the people I know are late for luncheons, business appointments, and weddings. Hell, they'd even be late for their own funerals. Me, I have to be everywhere five or ten minutes early." He went on to say, "And all of this wouldn't be that big of a problem if I didn't rage at them. According to the anger

(continued from 120)

workshop I took with you, I use sarcasm, put-downs, and fully interrogate the person who is late. I say things like, 'Well, I'm glad you finally decided to show up.' I said that to my wife just yesterday. I went on to say, 'You must have been talking to your mother again and I know whatever you two had to say was more important than being on time.' I guess I slipped into the "poor me" or martyr role there, didn't I? What is this all about? I'm ready to work on this."

Rob and I jumped right into the six TDM questions. It turns out when Rob was six, his father took him to the movies one Saturday morning at 10:00 a.m. when the theater opened. His father told him he'd be back at exactly 6:00 p.m. and that Rob had better be standing on that sidewalk waiting for him because if he had to come into that theater and get him, he'd regret it, which in Rob's case meant a severe whipping. As Rob regressed back to that time, he sobbed the way a little boy would who had to sit in a dark theater for hours waiting under the weight of such a threat. "I must have gone to the candy counter a thousand times to ask the woman there what time it was because I didn't want to be late and get a whipping, which now I really know was a beating and that 'whipping' us just a euphemism," he said in between sobs.

When Rob finished the session he said, "Whew! Where did that come from? I hadn't thought of that in decades. I'm sure there's more work to be done around this but I feel like I know and feel where some of my compulsivity comes from. Every time someone is late, I guess I say to them what I wish I could have said to my father in one way or another. Where have you been? Wasn't I important?" A couple more Detours followed and Rob actually was late for an appointment with me. You should have seen the smile on his face as he walked through the door.

This second question is an opportunity to go safely back in time; it may take from 5 to 15 minutes to remember what past experience the current situation is bringing up. And let me stress the word *safely*.

Many people think if they reawaken or disturb these old feelings, wounds, memories, or traumas, they might not only get bitten by them, they might even die. Remember, regressed people tend to overdramatize and blow things out of proportion. I tell people the pain has already occurred; talking about it, feeling it, getting to be able to let out words, emotions, and energy about it, begins the healing of it.

3. **What would you like to have said or done in the past but couldn't, for any reason? Say it now.** This is the opportunity you've been waiting for, perhaps for years or even decades. There are words that you had to swallow, feelings you had to stifle (often out of self-preservation), or the person you wanted to say these things to was for some reason incapable of hearing you. Basically, what this does is to facilitate emotional and psychological closure.

In twenty-five years of counseling and coaching, I bet I've heard, "I wish I had said," or "If only I had done," maybe a thousand or more times. These "wishes" and "if onlys" rattle around in the body, mind, and soul sometimes for decades. When people's emotional memory is activated around similar situations or statements made by someone in the present, they will often grab the fleeting opportunity to say what they couldn't say thirty years before, however inappropriate it is to the present time. That's how desperate we all are for closure.

This is why I refer to regression as a "present-person/people eraser." We erase the one(s) in front of us and replace them with a father, mother, former partner, or ex-boss and we say or do to them what we wanted to say or do to that other person or people but could not. Thirty or twenty years ago perhaps, we were angry or hurt by something that other individual said or did; now, the anger or hurt resurfaces as rage and we have all this re-pressed energy, plus opportunity, and we "let them have it," "blow them out of the water," "unload"—unpack the luggage of the past—right into the present person or people's lap. This very often elicits the question from such recipients: "Where is all of this coming from?"

4. **After saying what you wished or wanted to say back then, what would you have liked to have said or done to you?** To achieve true closure, we need not only to say the things we wish we could have said, but may need to hear something that we didn't hear then.

If you craved an apology, praise, appreciation, or validation at some time in your past, you may go to extremes. You may employ exhaustive efforts to get this from a present boss or spouse, and if it is not forthcoming, regression and rage may be the result. Now it is finally your turn to literally create the words and responses that would have healed you, had you heard them. This is self-directed healing par excellence.

Melvin said one day during a TDM session, "I always wanted my father to be proud of me, but he never seemed to be. I worked and worked and finally made millions with my construction business. I bought a brand-new Cadillac Escalade; my dad always thought that anyone who drove a Caddy had really made it in life. I drove up in his front yard and told him to get in, that I wanted to take him for a ride. John, you know that old fellow told me how proud he was of me, and all it did was make me so angry I could hardly see how to drive us home. It was like I was blinded by my rage. What he said didn't make me feel better at all. It made me feel worse."

We took the Detour and discovered that it was the Melvin of twelve and thirteen who needed those words from his father, not the forty-year-old man. When his seventy-year-old father praised him, it triggered the emotional memory of the times he had needed his dad's support as a child but never received it.

"What would you like to have him say or do back then?" I asked him. "Tell me you are proud of me even though I failed the seventh grade and that you're not ashamed of me and that you'll help me," he said as he used one of the emotional-release techniques of twisting a towel—letting the old, unhealthy anger and rage out of his body.

5. **After saying what you needed to say and asking for the words or actions you needed back then, how are you feeling now?** The answers vary to this question but here are some of the standard ones most often heard after a successful TDM is taken: "I feel much lighter, like a load has been lifted off my shoulders," "I have more energy," or "I can't believe the present is so connected to the past." The past is too heavy for most of us to carry all alone, especially if that burden has been hoisted on our back for days, years, or decades. Other statements often

made by those who took the guided trip down memory lane will say things like, "It seems like my thinking is clear and now I know what I need to do in this present situation or person" or "I can now see clearly that I have choices."

6. **Do you still need to speak to the person or people who triggered your regression or rage?** For about seven out of ten people who completed TDM, the answer is, "No, I don't. This was more about me and my history than it was about me and them." Sometimes the answer is, "Yes, I do. I owe them an apology for my inappropriate reactions." Sometimes the answer is "Yes, I still need to talk to them. I am angry or hurt, but now I can do so appropriately.

   If the answer is yes, I encourage you to apply the Three-Minute Rule. This is a guideline for expressing anger appropriately in a present situation or to a present person. The rule is, if you think or feel it is going to take more than three, four, or maybe five minutes at the most to tell someone how you are feeling after having done TDM, it is probably because you are still confusing past with present and you may need to go back through the questions.

   Many times, the answer to question 6 is, "Next time, I just need to set a good boundary or know my limits in similar situations."

The Detour Method and Boundaries, Limits, Anger, and Rage

Would you like to reduce the number of times you become angry by 50 to 80 percent? Adults can reduce anger and rage

significantly by understanding and employing healthy boundaries and functional limits. Adults can minimize the anger and
rage in their children by teaching them how they, too, can establish boundaries and set limits. This is accomplished by modeling, because as we know saying, "Do as I say," isn't nearly as
powerful as saying, "Do as I do."

Children and adults alike learn by repetition and by mim-
icking what others do. However, the best way to communicate
the idea of boundaries to adults is to tell, show, and have them
practice. That's how they learn. It's not any different to teach
limits.

Boundaries

Before boundaries can reduce anger and rage, a few things must
first be accomplished. We need to:

- Define boundaries
- Discuss the different kinds of boundaries that exist
- Understand boundary errors
- Explain boundary violations
- Identify boundary impairment
- Feel and express the anger that comes from your bound-
  aries not being respected in the past

First, a boundary is not a wall. Walls are put in place by
people who cannot or do not know how to establish boundaries.
You can tell the difference between a boundary and a wall by
looking at your family and friends to see if they have flat heads
from banging them against your walls or calluses on their hands

from trying to tear them down. Many of us know a lot about wall construction and little about boundary building.

WHAT BOUNDARIES DO

Boundaries are what help us to separate our thoughts and feelings from those of other people, including, but not limited to our parents, children, spouse, or friends. Boundaries help us figure out who we are and who we aren't. They show where we begin and end and where someone else does, regulating distance and closeness by establishing the appropriate psychological, emotional, and physical space between others and ourselves.

Healthy adults not only create their own boundaries, they also can and will respect others'. People who stay regressed most of the time do not have good boundaries, so they don't respect other people's, and anger and rage follow.

Boundaries are invisible, symbolic fences that make us good neighbors, partners, and parents, by protecting our body, emotions, heart, and soul. They can be placed around:

- Our physical being
- Our emotional life
- Our sexuality
- The words people say to us
- What information we allow in
- Our finances
- Our spirituality (and how to protect it)

Let's go through examples of each.

Proxemics is a term coined in 1966 by anthropologist Edward T. Hall to describe set, measurable distances between people as they interact. Hall states that different cultures maintain different standards of personal space. He found that there are four different types of space between people: intimate, personal, social, and public. Most people in the United States who have not had their physical boundaries severely violated tend to allow most people 4 to 7 feet of space when speaking to them in a social setting (for example, a party). In Latin cultures, that distance is smaller, as Latinos/Hispanics tend to be more comfortable standing close to each other; but in Nordic cultures, the opposite is true. People unfamiliar with each country's ideal personal space can make mistakes without even knowing it, while interacting with others of another culture. In addition to cultural differences, each person has a personal distance that is comfortable for him or her. When you are talking with a new person, you can usually see visual cues as to whether you are too close or too far for the individual's comfort—such as subtle changes in the pitch of the person's voice or whether he or she leans toward you or away from you.

Emotional boundaries can include how much or how little of someone's anger, sadness, fear, or joy you will allow to come toward you before you have had enough or before becoming overwhelmed. These emotional boundaries say, "Your anger or fear is yours, not mine," and vice versa.

Sexual boundaries in place can communicate, "It is all right for you to hold my hand but that is all," "You can put your arm around me but go no further," "You cannot talk about my sexuality, or talk to others about my sexual habits or preferences," or "You cannot touch my children sexually," and so on.

Informational boundaries say, "When I've had enough information about this or that subject or person, I don't want to hear or take in any more, because if I do I may get overstimulated," which for many people is very often a precursor to regression and later rage.

Financial boundaries say, "I will talk to my boss about how much he pays me." "I may talk to my father about what I paid for my home," or "My accountant and banker have access to my financial life, but I don't discuss it with acquaintances or social friends."

A word of caution: As with using any new tool in your emotional toolbox, the first time you use your boundaries and limits around unhealthy people, they will often react negatively. They may get very angry and even enraged or outraged with you and try to talk you out of your new psychological and emotional equipment for managing your life better: "You are just putting walls up between us," "Why are you not allowing me access to these parts of your life like you used to?" "You are becoming rigid," and so on. When they first encounter a person's setting of good boundaries, they may even question themselves: "Am I being too inflexible?" or "Are these really walls?" They will doubt their ability to create healthy boundaries. And very often in the beginning, their boundaries may be a little over the top because they will have gone from having no boundaries to setting boundaries everywhere, all the time.

Spiritual boundaries define what comes into my spiritual being: "I may let my minister talk to me and give me spiritual advice, solace, or comfort, but not people pounding on my door who want to lay out their religious strategies or dogma."

One of the reasons why establishing good, clear boundaries reduces anger—and therefore ultimately rage and regression— is because they can be highly effective in dealing with and negotiating stress, anxiety, conflicts, confrontation, and intimacy. Boundaries can reduce tension, friction, and misunderstanding. Believe it or not, they can also increase connection and comfort. If you know where you begin and end, and I know where I begin and end, we don't have to worry about encroachment, abandonment, invasion, or oppression.

To prevent turning boundaries into just another "technique" to put distance between yourself and those you are afraid of or don't want to be in a relationship with, it is important to know the difference between a healthy boundary and an emotional wall.

EMOTIONAL WALLS

- **The Barricade**—As opposed to healthy boundaries, which are flexible, this wall is too rigid. It is an immovable or intractable obstacle created by the new boundary maker that allows people to come too close and then tries to overcorrect themselves by requiring them to go too far away.
- **The Moat**—Here, people are kept at such a distance with a wall so broad that it keeps virtually everyone out of the boundary maker's life. Moats tend to isolate rather than protect and serve.

Boundary makers with this kind of wall have trouble connecting, with making and keeping friends, but with enough time and trust, they will open their gates and allow other people in.

- **The Road Block**—This is created by people who tend to be inflexible in their ways, habits, and preferences. They can't take in or receive new ideas or experiences outside their comfort zone. They tend to be legalistic, intolerant, and governed by rules.

- **The Picket Fence**—This is made by people who are too accommodating. These boundary makers always change their mind and never stick to anything. In contrast, healthy boundaries are like privacy fences that let people know how far they can come before they need to stop or ask permission to be allowed in further.

Brenda is married to a very controlling, old-fashioned husband. She recently discovered that he has been reading her e-mails for years, has had her phone tapped, and hired a private eye to follow her for the past six months. All of this stems from his extreme jealousy. He is fearful she will leave him as his first wife did. Brenda is afraid that her husband will leave her if she confronts him about this, so she allows this to happen without saying anything but she is full of rage for having done so.

Cheri lived with a man for three years. When they finally broke up, she requested that he change his mailing address and have all mail stopped being sent to her address. Five years later, his mail still goes to her address. He comes by every couple of months to pick it up, promising he will change the mailing address, but never does, even though Cheri's current husband has been the one on occasion to hand him his mail.

BOUNDARY ERRORS

How we defend our boundaries is as varied as the people who create them. But before we defend them, we must recognize when our boundaries are not honored either through boundary violations or boundary errors (a term coined by Anne Katherine).

Let's focus on the lesser offense of boundary error before we take on boundary violation. A boundary error comes about from lack of information or miscommunication or lack of cultural or social norms and customs. It is not intentional or malicious. And they very often occur because of lack of forethought. Regressed men and women tend to act on assumption, whereas emotionally healthy men and women tend to ask more questions.

Jennifer doesn't like to be kidded or teased about her prematurely gray hair. She's only twenty-one. Still, she receives unsolicited comments and "cute remarks" about her hair all the time. This would be a boundary error because she never told those making the comments that she wasn't comfortable hearing them. Talking too loudly with someone—error. Giving someone a hug without asking and then being told the person doesn't like to be hugged by strangers—boundary error.

BOUNDARY VIOLATIONS

A boundary violation is when people know that Jennifer doesn't like to be teased about her hair and they do it anyway. Being told that their volume is too loud and then speakers persist—violation. Having been told someone doesn't like to be hugged by strangers yet a person keeps pushing to do so—violation. Of course, there are much more serious violations than the above examples, but you get the picture.

How do you know when a boundary violation has taken place until you are really familiar and comfortable with yours and other's boundaries?

SIGNS OF BOUNDARY VIOLATION

If your boundaries have been violated, you may feel:

- Angry
- Betrayed
- Frightened
- Shamed
- Powerless
- Sad
- Anxious
- Unsafe

These feelings say someone has gotten closer to you physically, sexually, emotionally, and so on, than you are comfortable with. Or it they may point to the fact that your privacy has been invaded and you are not safe with the person or group that has crossed a boundary.

These signs can be identified as they are happening, but ideally it is best to become aware that you have these feelings before it's time to defend your boundaries. Clarifying what and where your boundaries are before they are invaded will minimize or even eliminate much of the discomfort that is associated with boundary violations.

As I said earlier, many people who have little or no experience setting and defending boundaries resort to the "distancer" form of rage. If you can't maintain or defend your boundary, you may find yourself keeping your distance from the person or group that you are letting cross it, or you may keep people at a distance with your wall of unavailability; which very often is a trigger for their regression and rage.

Another unhealthy way to avoid setting and defending boundaries is to lock yourself into one of many roles people play. Remember, where there are roles there is rage.

No one can really get close to people who play or are labeled such roles as:
- The hero
- The designated problem
- The clown
- The peacemaker
- The boss
- The baby of the family

The hero never feels seen, or fears appearing vulnerable; the designated problem diverts other problems from being resolved; the clown is never taken seriously; the peacemaker never feels appreciated; and so on.

HOW TO SET BOUNDARIES EFFECTIVELY
If you don't use distance, roles, rage, and walls, what do you do? You learn to say and mean the following words and statements

that many people never say (and mean) except perhaps only a few times in their lifetime: No! No more! Enough! Stop!

If "No!" is not respected as a complete sentence, then anger and finally rage follows. The famous or infamous Gestalt therapist Fritz Perls said, "If you can't say 'No,' then your 'Yes' doesn't mean a damn thing." A person who cannot say no is constantly playing the role of the "yes–man" (or-woman), to the detriment of his or her own physical, emotional, and spiritual well-being. Why is it so difficult to say, "Stop, I don't want to hear any more," or "No more!" or "Enough!"? Because most who can't say these words regress back to a time, usually childhood, when these words were not allowed or our primary role models could not use them successfully and without negative consequences.

There are other ways to stop and defend boundary violations, encroachments, and invasions that will reduce anger and rage radically:

1. Identify the specific violation: "When you don't knock before coming into my room . . . "
2. Tell the person how you feel to have your space, needs, and feelings disrespected: " . . . I get angry and scared . . . "
3. Add energy, body language, and sterner words: " . . . and I'm serious about this," while putting up your hand in a stop motion or planting your feet firmly.

Know what you will do and won't do, should the violation continue or occur again. It is important that you *know*, but it is very important that you don't *tell* another adult.

If you convey the consequences to adult violators verbally, they will more often than not regress (although they probably already are regressed if what they have said or done is not a boundary error/mistake) and then hear you making "threats" or giving them "ultimatums," which then will further their regression and trigger their fight (the most common response), flight, or freeze reaction.

However, you should tell children what the consequences will be should they violate or disregard your boundaries, so they can learn to make healthy choices in the future.

DEFENDING BOUNDARIES

An important part of setting good boundaries is able to stick with them and defend them appropriately when necessary. A few months ago, I was teaching a workshop on boundaries, limits, and anger. About three hours into the presentation, after hearing me say for the third or fourth time, "A boundary that can't be defended is not a real boundary but just a really good idea," Tom raised his hand and said, "I set good boundaries with my mother when I go to see her but she refuses to acknowledge them. But it's not because I don't have them; she just ignores them."

"Then they're not really boundaries, because real boundaries can't be ignored. Think of the fence around your house. If you don't open the gate, or tear down the fence, or let your neighbors tear it down, then they can't come into your space. Do you agree?" I asked him.

"No, I don't. Let me give you a personal example and you'll see what I mean. I set a boundary and she ignores it and then I get very angry. Well, no, to be honest I get enraged. See, I go over for dinner every Sunday. She's all alone, now that my father is dead. We sit down and I put on my plate what I want and then she puts food on my plate that she wants me to eat, like Brussels sprouts, which I hate. I tell her I don't want them and I don't want her to put food on my plate, that it's my plate!" He paused.

"So what happens?" one of the workshop participants asks.

Tom continued his story. "She puts the food on every time. I set a boundary and she ignores it every time, so it's not that I don't make boundaries clear."

I asked Tom, who owned his own auto repair shop, how old he was.

"I'll be thirty-two next month. What has that got to do with anything?" You could hear the irritation in his voice.

"What do you want me to do?" he said, his face red with anger, "Throw the food in her face? She's my mother, for Christ's sake."

"No, that would be rage, not defending a boundary."

Another workshop participant offered this suggestion. "How about saying something like, 'Mom, if you keep putting food on my plate, I'm leaving.'"

From all the nodding in the room, I could tell most of the workshop participants liked that idea, but it wasn't the right choice either. "No, that's a threat," I said.

Most of the people I've worked with over the years that have boundary and anger issues tend to think there are really only two ways to defend a boundary. One is to leave the person who tends to ignore their boundaries or do something like what Tom said, "Throw the food in her face" or some other violent or aggressive act.

So what would be a good way for Tom to defend his boundaries with his mother? The next time he speaks to her, he could say, "Mom, I won't be coming home for Sunday dinner anymore. I'll be coming over on Sunday afternoon for tea only." Or, "Mom, I've already eaten, I'll sit here and watch you eat." If she asks him why not, he can answer, "When I'm eating with you, I don't feel respected."

Those are just a couple of the choices Tom has. Remember, when we're not regressed we can see our options past fight or flight, but Tom's vision was clouded and obviously his issue with his mother was longstanding.

Limits

Limits are even more of a mystery to the majority of people than are boundaries. Even professionals confuse boundaries with limits—if they discuss them with their clients at all. There is a huge, important difference and knowing it will reduce anger, rage, and regression significantly.

In a nutshell, a boundary says to another person or group, "This is how close you can come to me."

A limit is your emotional and intellectual knowledge of how far *you'll* go with a situation, condition, marriage, job, parent, or child.

Many people have trouble knowing what their limits are both in personal and professional circumstances. Mildred, a very compassionate and thoughtful mother and owner of a resale

clothing store, called me, very upset and angry. "I
with my son, I don't know what to do," were her first word
"Hello." "I told him I would put him through two alcohol a
drug treatment programs and then he's on his own."

"How is that going?" I asked.

"Not too well. That is why I'm so mad at him. I have now put him through four expensive treatments at the best centers in the country."

"Mildred," I said, "what are your limits?"

She fired back, "I said two. But obviously it wasn't. That's why I'm so angry."

"So you don't know your limits and you're angry with him because he doesn't know them, either?"

Mildred laughed and said, "Oh!"

When people don't know what their limits are, and then with hindsight see they've gone way beyond them, they tend to get angry or enraged at the other person or the situation because they've been pushed beyond their comfort level.

Matthew is a short, stocky man who works with his hands, which are as big as a catcher's mitt. He called me, saying he wanted to work on how he says too much to the wrong people and not enough to the right people, but mostly because he wanted to know why he can't say no to a woman.

"Several weeks ago, I had a date with a beautiful woman," Matthew said. "We were sitting at Starbucks, drinking coffee, when she asked me why my wife and I got divorced. I got very anxious and I didn't want to tell her, but I proceeded to try to explain the reasons. 'Why did I do that?' was all I kept asking

Matthew didn't want to tell a
.....use it wasn't time to do so yet and
....but he disregarded it. He had no
...e in this and many other situations.
....most of us were taught very little

...y, "I saw my mother go way beyond
her limits, regarding .... ather's verbal abuse. I saw my dad go
way beyond his limits, regarding work. I watched him work
eighty and ninety hours a week."

Setting limits can actually lead to deeper connection with
those we care about. Because we don't know our limits, we go
much further or stop very short of where we want to be and how
much we want to be with or how much we want to do for such
people.

In situations like Matthew's, not knowing our limits is a main
factor in turning us into "care takers" instead of care givers.
Care givers have good boundaries and know their limits. Care
takers go way beyond and further than they really want to go.
Care takers actually end up taking something out of those they
are around—such as their integrity, energy, self-esteem, or the
money they find underneath the cushions on the couch or lying
around. In other words, we have to take something for giving up
something of ourselves that we really do not want to give. Many
people who don't know or pay attention to their limits tend to
feel resentment and therefore need some kind of payment or
restitution. However, people who know and respect their own
limits can care for others without resentment, without feeling as

if something is being taken from them, and they actually feel energized by their giving to others. This is what I call being "compassionately assertive," which I'll say more about later.

When we listen to our own internal rhythms for closeness and separateness, we know what our limits are to be with someone before resentment, regression, or remorse sets in. If we stay true to our rhythms, we know how long we can visit our parents without falling into odd, destructive conversations and patterns. If we know when to seek solitude to recharge our batteries, we won't have to push people away or run away from a relationship just because we can't say, "I need some time alone."

I asked another client of mine named Terry, who was taking a sabbatical from interacting with his father, how long he thought he could be with him when he resumed the relationship before regressing. "Maybe thirty minutes, and then I'll become his little boy again who stays much longer with his daddy and we'll be in the same old dysfunctional drama we're always in."

"How about just staying thirty minutes or less, if that is your limit?" I asked.

"You mean, go with my rhythms for closeness and separateness? But his feelings will get hurt if I just stayed thirty minutes. And what if I left and then he died before I went back?"

I forgot to mention Terry acts in community theater now that he's retired as president of a bank in Chicago. "Well," I said, "If you stay longer, what happens?"

"We almost always get testy and irritable with each other," he said.

"And if you went with your limits?"

"We'd probably enjoy each other's company. I'd leave on a good note because I'd still be an adult instead of a pissed-off kid who didn't want to ever come back and see his father for a long time."

Limits not only help us establish the difference between care giving and care taking; they separate quantity from quality. Terry recognized that if his father did die, it would be after a *compassionate* exchange of time, energy, respect, and love, not after a *resentful* one.

Here are a few more examples of less dramatic ways to think about limits:

- I'll only be able to go one more week.
- I'll explain this two more times.
- I can talk about this for thirty minutes.
- I'll give my boss one month to respond to my request.

Let's recap. The adult who is not regressing can easily set boundaries and limits that can be pulled in, extended, or shifted, based on choice, new information, or more experience, depending on the individual situations and people. Our boundaries and limits are clear to us and to those we live with, love, or work with. Good boundaries and limits help the adult not only reduce incidents or anger, rage, and regression, but also protect us without isolating or pushing other people away. They fe distance so that we don't have to accept anyming, or abusive words, actions, or demeaning

Good boundaries and limits actually increase intimacy, clarity, communication, and vulnerability because you can say no when you need to. You can also say yes when you want to. You know where you stand and let others know more about you. It enhances other people's feelings of safety and trust because they can rely on you when you say: "No more," "Enough," "Stop," or, "It's okay, you can come closer." When we don't compromise our boundaries and limits, no matter what someone may think, and stay true to ourselves, everyone involved wins in the long run, in any relationship. You may find yourself behaving and feeling healthier every day, lessening your need to take the Detour and taking less time with the Detour when you do need it.

Why TDM Will Work for You

I developed The Detour Method twenty-five years ago to create a safe, self-help way to experience and express emotions deeply and appropriately for the tens of thousands who don't necessarily feel that professional therapy is right or really not necessary, useful, or affordable. It is based on simple, down-to-earth principals for living a physically and emotionally healthier life. TDM helps the one taking the detour separate rage from anger and take him or her gently into past memories and feelings and then gracefully back into the present, before going to confront a person or group. By virtue of taking the Detour, the emotional charge a person has around a heated or intense discussion is dissipated and reduced to a manageable level.

TDM is a tried and proven process that helps the person detach, diffuse, and discharge excess energy, emotion, and confusion, leaving participants with an easier and clearer way to communicate.

The six questions mentioned earlier and the elicited responses give the one taking the Detour time to "take a deep breath," "count to ten," "sleep on it," or "clear their heads;" all things that we've been told to do since childhood, before doing or saying something we most likely will regret later. The difference is The Detour Method is giving the person several opportunities to do more than such passive suggestions as "count to ten"; it engages the individual mentally, physically and psychologically.

At the beginning of my workshops I tell participants that if I trigger something in them, they should take the Detour with an assistant first. Then, if they still need to talk to me, I'll make myself available.

The following is a recounting of a somewhat typical Detour scenario as told to me by Connie Burns, a senior trainer and social worker who cofacilitates many of my workshops.

Sherry, a very tall, big-boned blonde in her midforties, attended a four-day Anger Solution intensive. At the beginning, she agreed (as did all the workshop participants) that should she, for any reason, wish to abruptly leave before the conclusion of the program, she would spend a few minutes with an assistant and take the Detour.

On the third day, Sherry stood up during the afternoon session and sprinted out of the room. Her face and neck were flushed and she was very upset. Connie went out after her and asked her what was wrong. Sherry said she was leaving the workshop because she was mad, upset, and disappointed. "John is using and encouraging others to use language that I, as a born-again Christian, am not going to tolerate."

Connie said Sherry went on like this for another ten minutes or so, venting and crying as she shook with fear.

Connie asked her, "Would you be willing to take a few minutes in the privacy and safety of your hotel room, to answer TDM's six questions?"

Hesitantly, Sherry agreed to try that. She went back to her hotel room and asked herself the six questions, one at a time, writing her answers on a piece of paper. After finishing the first question, "Does this remind you of anyone or any time in your past?" she started sobbing. When Sherry was a little girl, she would frequently visit her grandparents who lived close by. Sherry's grandfather was a preacher in the Church of Christ in her hometown. She thought the world of him. He was the sweetest, kindest, gentlest man . . . until he drank. Then he'd curse at her and her grandmother, and it scared Sherry to death. She just wanted to run away but she couldn't. Sometimes she would hide under the bed for hours until he passed out. When he was sober, he was a saint.

She hadn't thought about that for years and yet the memories came flooding back with little effort. She asked herself the second question, "What do you wish you could have said or done back then?" Sherry wished she could said, "Grandpa, you are a man of God and you shouldn't be cursing and yelling and scaring me and Grandma. I want you to stop drinking!" Then she would have left, she thought, as she wiped her tears with the palms of her hands.

"What do you wish he had said if he could hear those words and feelings?" That was easy enough to answer. Sherry wished he'd apologized for scaring her and her grandmother. She also wanted him to say he would stop drinking. Then, that he'd ask for forgiveness.

She took a deep breath and asked herself the fifth question, "How are you feeling right now?" Sherry felt better, lighter, and not as scared. She couldn't believe she'd buried that memory for so long.

The final question was, "What do you need to say or do now with John or this seminar?" She smiled and sighed as she wrote that she wanted to get back to the group. The workshop was helping her and now she knew John was not her grandfather and the workshop room was a safe place to be.

What Happens When the Detour Is Not Taken

When regressed people do not or cannot take a Detour when powerful, disproportional feelings and emotions are present, it is because they are usually in denial or afraid. They deny their feelings; their tense, overreactive body; and their history or past. Denial is a tricky devil because, by definition, it is like a psychological and emotional catch-22: If I knew I was in denial, I wouldn't be in denial!

We all sail down the River of Denial during difficult times and thus we are all passengers in the same boat. Some of us have been in denial about the pain in the present. We become defensive when someone pushes a button that has the potential to blow us out of our state of denial. We defend our position, our walls, our emotional property, or baggage. Most of all, we defend the patterns we have created to exist with, cope with, and survive the hurt, anger, loneliness, or fear in us.

These patterns of behavior, our ways of thinking and talking, were usually employed early on in our childhood. We saw these patterns—denial, defensiveness, aggressiveness, withdrawal, and many others—appear to help others survive unhealthy relationships, intense arguments, or dysfunctions of all kinds. We incorporated these patterns into our own arsenal of ways to defeat or defend against harsh words or abusive, destructive behavior. And, you know, they sort of worked, so we continue to hold on tightly to them even though they may have stopped working (if they ever did) a long time ago.

Stacey said he saw his father "storm out of the house whenever he and mom would argue and fight. I always thought he was a coward and I told myself I'd never do that to someone I loved." He paused and took a deep breath. "I do it all the time with my wife. I look back and see he was doing what I'm doing and that's just trying to get a little relief. But now my second wife says if I keep walking out when we're arguing, that one day when I come home I might find the house empty. I've got to get out of this pattern, but I don't know how. And there's even a small part of me that still doesn't let go of this pattern, because leaving has always made me feel in control. Sometimes it's the only way I know to feel safe."

The function of these defensive, reactive patterns is to create the illusion of control and safety. Think of these behavioral patterns like the grain in a piece of wood. We've all heard the sage advice, "Don't go *against* the grain, go *with* it." That works great

with wood, but not with regressive patterns of relating or interacting with others. These emotionally defensive patterns are
like the little channels rain makes in your yard or the big ones
in the Grand Canyon—the more rain, the deeper those channels; and soon, like the Grand Canyon, they become very difficult to get out of—not impossible, but just difficult, especially
until they are identified and one is consciously aware of them.
Just as the wood or the rain is not conscious of itself, the defensive patterns we resort to using are mostly unconscious.

The Detour Method helps people recognize the patterns they
are in and to go against them, or as I say—cut across the grain—
of their behavior, actions, and thought processes. By now, everyone knows the definition of insanity: "Doing the same thing over
and over again and expecting different results." Cutting across
the patterns yields different results and sometimes it is just this
that keeps us from going against our patterns—that we don't
know what will happen. Change is scary to many people. Well-
worn paths give us the illusion and semicomfort that we not only
know where we are going but at least we know where or what
someone else will go, say, do, or not do.

In my coaching sessions, I have asked this question to thousands of people: "What would happen if you_____?" You
can fill in your own blanks. I'd ask, "What would happen if you
told your father how angry you are and have been at him?" The
answer would be, "Well, I know he would _____."

"How do you know this?" I'd ask.

"I just do," they would say. "I know my father," which is code
for, "I know his patterns, or at least I tell myself I do, and I know
my own."

"Have you ever told him how angry you are in an appropriate manner?" I ask Shane, during one of his Detour sessions. "Well, no, not exactly. I mean, I've yelled at him before, though it doesn't do any good. I stopped seeing him or talking to him for a few years. That didn't change anything," said Shane. "I guess I don't really know what I'd say or do if I just got all of my rage out, as you suggest, and just sat down with him, man-to-man, and told him how I felt." He looked up at the ceiling of my office. "Wow! That's pretty scary to think about."

When regressive patterns are broken, new behaviors, ways of talking, thinking, being, and interacting begin to emerge. When we go against the grain of well-worn behavior, sparks fly and these sparks can ignite new, healthier, more satisfying interactions. We become creative instead of regressed and reactive. We become who we really are instead a collection of unconscious patterns.

Chapter 6

Doing What It Takes to Come Out of Anger, Rage, and Regression

N ow that you have all the information and insights about anger, rage, boundaries, and TDM, you are ready to do whatever it takes to keep you acting, thinking, talking, and making decisions like the powerful adult you know you are and can be more of the time. In this chapter, you'll discover the time-tested tools that literally thousands of people have tried. These tools are effective, efficient, and compassionate.

Five Keys to Bring You Back to the Present Moment

As mentioned earlier, if you are regressed, you can do TDM by yourself or with a facilitator who asks you the six questions. However, if you are doing this on your own and have finished asking yourself the questions but still feel something is missing, then you may need someone to employ one of the five follow-ing keys to bring yourself back to the here and now. They are:

1. Attention
2. Empathy
3. Time and time-out
4. Contact/connection when enraged or outraged
5. Discharge and emotional release

1. Attention

Attention is the first and most important of the five keys. With-out it, a person will stay in the past much longer. If you descend into the past, the attention key can bring you back if the emo-tional memory being triggered is not too traumatic and painful.

As with most good things, attention can also create a problem or two if not properly addressed. Many people don't know ex-actly how to give clear attention when someone is regressing and comes to them with a need for it. Men, in particular, tend to think the act of attention is more about giving feedback, of-fering suggestions, providing adequate counseling, helping, or coaching. And while TDM certainly employs and supports all of these, it is vital to clarify that genuine healthy attention will not include any of these until much later in the process. *Web-ster's Dictionary* defines *attention* as "the act of attending or heeding; the application of the ear to sounds, or of the mind to objects presented to its contemplation." If, with all the good in-tentions, I'm making suggestions, giving advice, or interrupt-ing, I am not attending or really hearing you. I am thinking about what I want to say, not about what you are saying.

It is also important to note that TDM is based on the principle that if someone is regressed and thus in a fight, flight, or freeze mode, you may be making the best suggestions, giving great feedback, or advising the person correctly on his or her options, yet the individual will not be able to take, assimilate, or act on them while regressed. The truth is, most regressed people won't be very appreciative of your efforts even if what you're saying is right.

The other problem with attention is that many people don't feel worthy of receiving it even from someone who knows how to give it. You will see this in certain therapy groups, 12-step meetings, or even in everyday conversations.

Charlie was in a men's therapy group I led for a weekend in New York. He had just recently received his divorce papers from his second failed marriage, had lost his best job ever, and was in terrible emotional turmoil. When it came time for him to share with the men what issues he wanted to work on, he said, "After listening to you guys talk, I don't think I have it that bad; clearly, several of you guys need the time, so I'll pass and that way there will be more for you." This was not arrogance but rather low self-esteem, low self-worth. It turns out Charlie just didn't feel worthy of mine and the group's attention even though he'd signed up for it.

In conversations, you might hear this lack of ability to receive attention expressed as, "Oh, I don't want to bore you with my problems," or "Enough about me tell me about you," or "No, really, it's no big deal," or "It's not worth mentioning." All of these can be code for "I can't accept the attention you are offering."

What does attention look like and sound like? Attention is quiet, often wordless connection, palpable to the point of being intense. The attention-giver using TDM is in the present moment and is actively listening—not passively hearing—the regressed person. Active listening is much more than merely hearing the words coming out of the mouth of the angry, hurt, or disappointed person speaking. The active listener engages with the speaker with his or her whole body.

The one providing good, clear, focused attention sits erect or perhaps leans into the one speaking. His or her eyes seldom leave the speaker. The active listener's breathing is full and deep into the diaphragm even though the regressed person might only be taking in shallow breaths due to the anxiety or fear that often accompanies regression. This deep breathing on the part of the one giving attention has a calming and soothing effect on the speaker. The full-bodied breathing says, "I'm here. I'm not going anywhere. I'm not regressing or getting triggered by anything you are feeling or saying." The regressed participant in the Detour process hears the attention-giver's breath going in and out and very often begins to breathe in sync with the other person. Now, if you do the Detour by yourself, it is important to pay very close attention to body sensations, your breathing, and the feelings, emotions, and pictures of people and places that may appear on your mental screen.

Attention becomes the solid ground the regressed person can stand on after almost drowning in the quicksand of the past. I can't stress the necessity of providing a person who is regressed with the power of attention.

2. *Empathy*

Empathy is the second most important element that must be given a good facilitator and extended to the regressed person taking the Detour, because it allows the latter to "feel" the attention; sometimes to the point of being freed of the regression on the spot. Without empathy, the regressed individual won't feel understood, which leaves that person feeling alone and isolated in his or her attempts to negotiate the past as it pertains to the present issue that triggered the regression. When people ask, as they often do, "Can't I do the Detour by myself?" I always reply, "Absolutely; however, there are just some things we can't really give to ourselves and one such thing is empathy." Remember that not all regressions require another person, especially if they are not too deep or debilitating.

Empathy is often confused with sympathy. Empathy can be defined this way: "I understand some of what you are saying because I've been through similar experiences myself." Note: I am not saying, "I know exactly how you feel" or "I've had exactly the same experiences." Neither comment is necessary for one to empathize with another person's rage, anger, pain, loss, anger, hurt, sadness, or disappointment.

Many people were taught that sympathy was what you provide the hurting man or woman. A client said to me during a session, "I feel my husband's sadness but when I tell him this he gets angry. I don't understand. He had a very painful childhood and you can see it on his face. I just feel so bad for him."

Good intentioned? Absolutely. Helpful? Not at all.

There are many problems with sympathy's being given to another adult. Someone who receives sympathy may often feel patronized or condescended to. To a regressed person, sympathy conveys the sentiment that the individual is not capable at a certain level to handle his or her own feelings and that the sympathizer is stronger, more resilient, and even superior in some way. Sympathy connotes, "There, there. I'll feel your pain for you. I'll take it on. My shoulders can carry the weight because yours cannot."

Now, don't misunderstand, sympathy is a wonderful gift of the spirit and heart of people. It's just not appropriate most of the time to give to another adult, especially when that person deeply desires to be seen, heard, and understood while descending into the past and desiring to share that with a listener. On the other hand, sympathy should be given to very young children and to those adults who, for whatever reason (brain injury, dementia, or Alzheimer's), cannot be cognizant of their own needs or cannot express them. When your young child hurts, naturally you will hurt. On their respective first day of school, your children will be scared and you will be scared, too. But when those children become teenagers who experience their first heartbreak or huge athletic or academic defeat and you tell them you feel what they feel, you should expect them to recoil from you, because sympathy says, "I feel what you feel, therefore we are one and the same. Teens needs to separate their feelings—whatever they are—from yours. Empathy would say, "You can get through this" or "I respect your adultness even though right now you may feel like a toddler, because I've felt something like this [not exactly] before. And look at me, I made it—and I know you can do the same."

In other words, sympathy shrinks an already regressed person, but empathy elevates. The regressed person just needs some attention and a little or a lot of empathy.

3. *Time and Time-Out*

Just as the contraction and expansion of time is a major indicator to the process of coming out of a regression and reducing rage, time can be the greatest friend a regressed person has—if used properly.

One of the best uses of time is what became popular in the late 1960s and '70s for managing disruptive behavior in children—the time-out. Many parents have used this discipline method successfully. It is employed when children are acting out or inappropriately, as a way to extract them from situations so they can collect themselves, reflect, and then be reintroduced back into their surroundings. This is a very important key that you can use by and on yourself as an adult.

What I propose in my trainings and consultations with people with anger/rage issues—or those who regress—is to put themselves in a time-out. In other words, I encourage them to withdraw from highly charged conversations or situations until they can collect themselves and allow for the dissipation of intense emotions. Taking some time allows the heated emotions to cool, the blood to flow back to the neocortex. Then the individuals can think, act, and talk like—and be—mature adults.

The best advice about time that I've ran across in the last twenty or so years comes from one of America's greatest poets—Wallace Stevens: "Sometimes the truth depends on a wall around the lake." If people don't take time to take a walk, drive to the country, stroll on the beach, or take a few moments in a quiet room, they may regret it. They may preach the gospel according to them and teach, criticize, or shame someone, thinking they are speaking their truth, only to find out later they weren't even close to evaluating or perceiving a situation, issue, or person correctly.

Time alone is not always sufficient to bring us out of a regression. People often ask me, "Can't you bring yourself out of regression?" The answer is absolutely—sometimes. At other times, we may find it necessary to request some time from a friend, colleague, parent, teacher, therapist, or facilitator of The Detour Method, so we can be the recipient of their attention and empathy. However, the minute people ascertain they are in a regression and take some time out of the triggering context, they may be halfway back into the present moment.

Regression and rage can be scary places to be by oneself. Regressed people may feel more like a three-year-old who sees monsters under the bed at night. They need to know they are safe and, most important, not alone.

We've all heard the cliché, "Time is of the essence," or perhaps we are familiar with another poet's words: "Time for indecisions and decisions and revisions"—T. S. Eliot.

4. Contact/Connection When Enraged or Outraged

Believe it or not, in most cases when people are raging, they are actually trying to make contact. At that time, even a negative or painful connection is better than loneliness or isolation. Rage then becomes an attention-seeking behavior. The child who pulls the lamp off the table not only watches to see if it cracks but is also observant of whether anyone is watching. That child is much like the man in the restaurant who is verbally abusive to the waiter or waitress and is unconsciously making a scene so he can be in the spotlight, if not as a hero, then as a villain, which is better than no attention at all.

In this very highly populated world of ours, connection is rare. To really connect with another has become an all-but-dying art. Neighbors go for years without introduction. Colleagues sit in the next office cubicle and never speak. Grandparents live alone three thousand miles away from family. Fathers and mothers now working more hours than ever hardly see their children, and have little or no time for friends or each other.

If you recall, isolation and loneliness are preconditions for regression. Contact with one's deepest self and memories or feelings can be accomplished by taking the time to walk or taking the Detour using pen and paper. Sometimes, contact with another human being, especially another of the same gender, can bring the regressed adult out of rage and regression. The question is, What kind of contact? It can be:

- Eye to eye
- Face to face
- Hand to hand
- Side by side

Even telephone contact with another works for many. A soothing, calm voice on the other end of the line can work wonders.

However, I almost never suggest e-mailing or text-messaging when regressed, and that includes even e-mailing a good friend who knows you can be easily misinterpreted and misunderstood. Without tone, facial expression, and body language, electronic contact alone is easily misconstrued.

Touching a regressed person at just the right moment can wake up the sleeping adult inside him or her, so long as that touch is safe and appropriate. Studies have shown touch increases blood flow, especially to the brain. It helps the brain to release soothing chemicals: neuropeptides, serotonin, oxytocin, and others. It even raises the T-cell count. Unfortunately, touch can also be a trigger for many people's unpleasant, painful, and even traumatic emotional memories. If a person is regressed and he or she is touched inappropriately by a well-intentioned friend or acquaintance, it can exacerbate the regression, not elevate it. For this reason, I qualify touch and encourage the person who is trying to administer attention, empathy, and give some time, to ask or say to the regressed person:

- Do you like to be touched?
- How would you like to be touched?
- Is the touch right? (soft enough, tender enough, strong enough, and so on)
- I can stop as soon as you want me to.

One of the problems with touch is that many good-hearted people will touch others who are in pain the way they, themselves, would want to be touched in a similar situation—in sympathy, rather than with empathy. This is why it is important to ask first, and not insist on touching someone who refuses physical contact . . . and to not take a no as a personal rejection.

Regression can be a very frightening state. Regression loves company. When people are regressed, most don't want to be all alone in their past, so they trigger another person's emotional memory—usually someone they are close to—just so they won't be alone. Even though most people can do TDM on their own, in some cases coming out of a regression requires company. Physical contact, employed with sensitivity, can reinforce their connection with the present and feel reassuring.

5. *Discharge and Emotional Release*

The fifth key in the process of coming out of our past and out of regression is discharge and emotional release. Although attention, empathy, time, and contact are often enough to spring us from the prison of our past, it is discharge and emotional release that dramatically decreases the likelihood of returning to those particular traps.

Discharge and emotional release can be achieved by anyone who will exert time, energy, and pay attention to the memories, feelings, and emotions that arise while doing the Detour alone. Add some information, tools, and techniques to the mix, and the person can let go of a great deal of anger, rage, or sadness. It can be achieved also by getting attention, empathy, and contact from a safe person and using TDM's six-question process to discover the distress one is feeling around issues in the past that are still being triggered in the present.

Discovering and uncovering distress is like being a psychological and emotional archaeologist. Buried in our emotional history are the ancient memories, repressed feelings, words, and actions we had to hide from others and even ourselves. We must carefully brush these off once discovered, examine them closely, and name them—betrayal, rage, abandonment, abuse, belittlement, hurt, sadness, anger, disappointment, and so on. Once we have gently dug into and around these broken shards of our past and named them, we must see how they fit into our overall life picture. Like a cultural anthropologist, the facilitator of TDM must remain detached from the culture of pain and hurt if he or she is to be an effective guide into and out of what can be for many an emotional heart of darkness (at the most extreme end) or out of a just slightly uncomfortable emotional state.

We might think of our past as being littered with little firecrackers . . . or atomic bombs. TDM is a process of diffusing those bombs so they won't go off in the middle of a conversation with a spouse, friend, or colleague. Attention, empathy, time, and contact can achieve this most of the time, but some bombs are so old, rusty, and corroded that they have to be discharged safely. This is where emotional release comes into the picture.

When people need to feel an emotion—whether it be anger, sadness, fear, hope, or joy—and they can't express it at the moment it is felt, that emotion becomes a "frozen residue of energy that has not been resolved and discharged," according to Peter

Levine in *Waking the Tiger*. He goes on to say, "This residue remains trapped in the nervous system where it can wreak havoc on our bodies and spirits."

We've all heard the phrase, "It will melt your heart." TDM and its use of attention, empathy, time, and contact helps to thaw out these frozen feelings and allows them to be finally released after being stored in deep freeze within our body.

This flowing, discharging, emotional release allows the anger, tears, and fears to come out; sometimes slowly, sometimes quickly. More often than not, people can release their emotions on their own, but sometimes it helps to have a facilitator, someone safe who will not be afraid of how big your emotions and/or discharge may get.

When you feel the need to use a facilitator, it is the safety they give you that allows you to open up. Harvey Jackins, the creator of Co-counseling or Re-evaluation Counseling, as it is often called, says, "The distressed human spontaneously seeks to claim the aware attention of another human. If he is successful in claiming and keeping this aware attention of another person, a process of discharge ensues." But remember, everything must be first grounded in catching regression and actively seeking a safe person's attention, because as Jackins goes on to say, "Discharge . . . requires time for completion."

Discharging your anger appropriately and thoughtfully is called "anger work." It can be done alone or with a safe person. The following section will guide you through exercises you can do just about anywhere.

Anger Work You Can Do at Home or in the Office

Taking a detour leaves you more aware that the burning issue has cooled off, because it is more about you and your history than about the current situation. TDM puts things into their correct perspective and gives you calm and clarity.

There are many different techniques/exercises that work for different people. Following are several that have a high rate of success. Try one that sounds comfortable for you.

Write It Down

1. Set aside 5 to 10 minutes.
2. Sit down, take out some paper or a journal and a pen or pencil.
3. Remember to take full deep breaths during this process as this allows emotions to flow more fluidly.
4. Write, with your nondominant hand, one to three letters saying what you feel toward or wish you could have said to a person, event, or situation that triggers your anger.
5. Hold nothing back; neither editing nor censoring is allowed, just let it flow out of you.
6. Then take each letter, tear or wad it up, and throw it across the room or into the garbage can.
7. Take a full, deep breath and repeat as necessary.

Using the hand you wouldn't normally use to write a letter allows you to go to more simple language, more emotion because you use different parts of your brain and body. You are writing the way the hurt child might talk instead of like a sophisticated, educated adult. The emotional release and discharge that comes from each heartfelt word reduces the tension and stress, so that now you take the pen with your dominant hand and write a fresh, appropriate "angry" letter if you still feel the need to do so.

As you have seen by now, taking a detour allows you to see the current issue in its correct perspective. But now if you still need to send a letter to the person you are angry at, your pen will not be poisoned. You won't have to fear negative reactions, had you not first gotten your rage out. You may still have a negative response if the person you are sending it to is regressed. But you won't be afraid because you're not regressed.

The Twister

1. You can sit or stand for this technique.
2. Go to a private, safe place, making sure the person or group that triggered your regression and rage is nowhere around or at least out of earshot.
3. Take a bath towel and stretch it out lengthwise, bringing your hands close to the center, and begin twisting it while thinking about what made you feel the disproportional feelings that are flooding your body and brain. The more you feel, the harder you twist.
4. If no one can hear you, then begin talking, saying what you would like to have said, asking for whatever for any reason you couldn't.
5. Keep twisting until that bath towel becomes knotted up, releasing the knot in your stomach, the tension in your jaw, the tightness in your shoulders.

After several minutes of doing the Twister, take a look at the twisted towel, which represents the tension you're holding in your body. Our body often feels more like a twisted towel than like the towel in the bathroom shelf or the one we hold in our relaxed hands. A twisted body or towel cannot absorb the tension and stress of some days. The more anxiety, stress, pressure or trauma, the more our insides twist. Once we release and discharge the pent-up feelings, our body feels more like the soft, stretched-out towel that comes fresh out of the dryer ready to comfort and absorb the shocks, stains, and pains of everyday life.

Talking Pictures

1. Take photos from early or late childhood, or pictures of those who broke your heart or bank account, and position them so you can look at them.
2. Let the residual feelings come up—the anger, rage, or resentment.
3. Then say to them what you feel, what you wanted to say but couldn't, or even things actually said when you were with them but never felt had been heard.
4. Take out these photos of the phantoms of your past every day, as long as your anger needs release, knowing that these are representations of the past person, not the present one.

This anger work actually helps you separate the past person from the present one. James talked to the pictures of his ex-wife for a couple of weeks. "I spent fifteen to twenty minutes a day talking to the young woman I married twenty years ago. And the more I got off my chest, the easier it was to see her when I'd go pick up the kids for the weekend. Before this type of anger work, I'd walk into her new home where she lives with her new husband and I'd say something either to her or him that I'd later regret. My kids kept telling me they hated seeing us fight when we were married but it seemed worse now that we are divorced.

"After talking to her pictures and writing her a few letters that I never sent, we're not arguing at all. The truth is, I'm getting to know my kids' stepfather and I kind of like him! I guess this stuff really works."

Punching Pillows

1. Pounding overstuffed pillows is good anger-release work. No one can get hurt if no one is around to see the rage being released.
2. Hitting the bed with an old tennis racket releases rage from the muscles as well as the mind.
3. Screaming into pillows or in your car with the window rolled up also releases soothing chemicals in the brain.

I have suggested these anger-release work exercises to the many people who say they are numb, shut down, or don't feel their feelings because they have been so emotionally disconnected for so long. When they ask the typical question, "Why bother?" I answer, "Because movement creates emotion." People who are out of touch with their anger or rage can begin twisting a towel or hitting a pillow, and within five minutes or

168

so they actually begin to feel for the first time in weeks, months, or years.

Sitting in a comfortable chair trying to access deep-seated emotions just doesn't work for many. Sometimes after people try for three or four minutes and nothing is felt, they might say something like, "I'm just acting the part or I'm just faking it." My response is then, "Keep acting, keep faking it, because the emotions will come. At first, just focus on releasing the stress and tension you are holding in your body. So don't stop, keep going."

Remember, the goal of this kind of anger work is not only about physical release and discharge but also separating past from present and never hurting yourself or others in the process. When you complete any of the above exercises, ask yourself this question: "Did I get hurt?" "Did I hurt anybody?" The answer will always be no.

Many people have said to me before doing anger work, "I have tried to let him (or her, or the past) go but I can't. I'm still holding on."

One of the main things people use to hold onto an ex, or a young father or mother or hurtful friend is their unexpressed anger and rage. This toxic emotion is like a thick rope we have tied to ourselves and others. We drag them into present relationships and someone will often say, "You are still holding on to your ex, mom, anger, rage, and it's hurting me and you."

It's not always easy to let go because sometimes the anger and rage is all that's left to connect us to that person or that memory, as painful as it is. After anger work, that connection breaks. What I tell folks who articulate this fear is that the rope of anger we cling to more often can become a fine thread of forgiveness that connects our heart to other hearts that we may still love or care about and opens us up to be more present and emotionally available to the people of today with whom we want to be with deeper in a relationship.

Emotional Release and Discharge

Emotional-release work—as it has come to be known—began when it was obvious that some clients do not respond to the traditional "talk therapy" or the "talking cure" first created by Freud. Part of the problem with talk therapy alone is that these frozen feelings and emotions didn't have an outlet for physical release. Talking is primarily intellectual and is emitted from the rational part of the brain. Emotions, memories, and feelings are also located in the body, in our cells, tissue, bones, and muscles.

Emotional release and discharge is based on releasing pent-up, stored energy. Anger is energy. Sadness is energy. Love, joy, hate, and fear are all energies that, if trapped in the body of a person for too long, are detrimental to body, mind, and soul. For a variety of reasons—from social conditioning to family prohibition—those energies/feeling have not been allowed to be experienced and expressed. This can and does have damaging, toxic, and even perhaps terminal consequences.

While I resist turning the magnificent human being into another metaphor, bear with me once again for a few moments. The body is like a new car battery. At first, it is fully charged, just like we are at birth, and ready to be used to propel your car and your life forward and, from time to time, backward. But should this battery that began, like us, full of untapped energy, sit for too long, that energy—while never completely disappearing—dissipates to the point it either has to be recharged or appears to have "died." Why? Because batteries, like boys and girls, are meant to charge, discharge, charge again, and discharge. If you observe animals frequently and closely, you will see that any kind of trauma that is experienced is always released only moments after the fall or other incident. They will shake their whole body and then move on. They release or discharge and are back fully in the present moment.

Forget anger and rage for a minute. Let's take an emotion we haven't discussed that much yet, but will do so in a later chapter—love. If love, the feeling and emotion that gives great joy and sustains us through the most distressing periods in our lives, is not discharged or emotionally released from time to time, that same love can turn into selfishness, narcissism, and coldness. Love, like anger or fear, is an energy that, if blocked, denied, or repressed, will seek an outlet—a healthy one or a not-so-healthy one.

Let's take Caitlin as an example of all this energy and emotional release. As a little girl, Caitlin loved to be touched as most healthy children do, but grew up in a stoic, repressed family were there was little or no touching going on. Her father was a "serious intellectual," according to her, and her mother had been molested as a teenager by an uncle. Caitlin became touch deprived and then touch starved, which led to her being an adult with a disproportional need for tactile connection. "I feel like I'm too needy and that I've always turned my boyfriends off because I always wanted then to stroke me, caress me, and hold my hand much more than any of them were capable of," she said between the tears. "And what I don't understand at all," said this attractive twenty-five-year-old graduate student, "is that I pick literally touch-phobic men to give me all these things, men who don't seem to even need to be touched very much, let alone crave it like I do." In the long run, Caitlin has developed a very exaggerated anger toward all men. Although she denies this, she did admit to me that many of her friends have told her that they could see her manifest anger at men.

So, on one hand, she admits she has a regressive, disproportional need to be touched. On the other hand, she is also aware that she picks exactly the wrong people to give it to her. It's as if the energy of touch that was not received as a child has turned against her and contributed in part to her unsatisfying relationships. If the pain, sadness, anger, and frustration Caitlin felt as a little girl at not getting touched and the damage that did to her self-esteem is not sufficiently excavated with the powerful tools of attention, empathy, time, and contact, she will not release her pent-up emotions—the anger and sadness she most assuredly felt. However, if over time she is able to access her buried emotions, this will help bring her adult need for touch into equilibrium and perhaps she will find a partner who will be able to meet her needs in present time.

Other Ways to Discharge and Release

- Crying or sobbing
- Angry shouting
- Writing
- Vigorous movement
- Lively and interesting talking (but not usually just by itself)
- Trembling
- Laughing
- Yawning
- Energized play

All of the above forms of emotional release are nonviolent, nonaggressive, and appropriate if they are carried out at a safe distance in private or with an objective facilitator, but usually not around the person or group that triggered the regression and the need to release. Different people need to discharge and release their emotions differently. Just like what regresses you doesn't bother in the least someone else—and what always triggers their regression doesn't affect you because each person's history is different, so are our body's ways of discharging emotion may be different. Do whatever works best for you.

Chapter 7

Dropping the Anger and Rage and Becoming Compassionately Assertive

I f regression and rage do not diminish when one is in a relationship, compassion disappears. Anger stored in our body for too long turns into passive behavior, passive/aggressive behaviors and actions, or just plain aggressive reactions to what people say or do in circumstances that we find difficult or impossible to cope with.

The point and purpose of separating anger from rage and turning it into adult responses, understanding regression, and knowing when and how to use TDM will be a key component to becoming more and more compassionately assertive.

Compassion is the act of showing mercy and gentleness and at the same time doing so with strength of character, by first extending these qualities to oneself and then to others. It is grounded in authenticity and integrity with ourselves, bringing us in touch with and articulating our needs and desires, and is one of the truest acts of self-care we can express.

When rage, unexpressed anger, and regression exist, we become combative, combustible, and controlling. We try to force ourselves and others to be what and who we think we should be. Compassion is active, bold, and forthright, and is the complete opposite of passive, which is inert, inactive, apathetic, and really not much of anything. I'm not talking about the passive resistance employed by Gandhi, King, or Thoreau. Their kind of behavior is very active and assertive. Nor am I talking about the kind of passivity spoken about in Eastern religions such as Taoism.

Asserting or being assertive is a positive affirmation of our rights, space, thoughts, needs, and actions. It conveys who we are at our core. It is generated out of increased self-worth and a strong sense of self. Assertiveness means inserting ourselves into the stream of life, which sometimes requires going with the flow but often demands that we swim upstream, going against current thought, fads, tastes, and opinions; but we do so with compassion for those who may be moving against us. We demonstrate compassion because as adults we are less concerned with winning at the expense of others, we're willing to be wrong and admit it when we are, and we're more interested in being happy with ourselves and our behaviors than "right" at our own or another's expense.

So what does compassionate assertiveness look like, sound like, and feel like to you and those you choose to interact with?

Being compassionately assertive begins with something I've addressed all during this book—becoming more and more aware of your emotions and then becoming so attached to them that you'll never neglect, swallow, stuff, or betray your feelings again.

However, equally important is to detach yourself from other people's feelings and emotions. Note that the word *detached* does not mean you disregard, disrespect, denigrate, or destroy anyone. Detaching is disengaging from what another is feeling or thinking about, to create a safe space for what you are feeling or thinking.

Detachment is talked about a lot in recovery circles, especially for those attending Al-Anon (for family and friends of addicts) or for codependents. In recovery, people are taught to "detach with love." It is not abandonment; rather, a conscious effort to separate yourself from the *problem*, not the *person*.

One of the most compassionate things anyone can do is mind one's own business. Your feelings and thoughts, needs and wants, likes and dislikes are yours and yours alone. When you encounter others that have different beliefs and goals, it is not your business to try to change their mind to become more like you. I have said many times in my workshops and lectures, "Most of what we think is our business is none of our business." When we fall into the age-old trip of minding someone else's business, we often end up acting aggressive, passive/aggressive, or passive, but seldom compassionately assertive.

Mary Beth monitors her eighty-six-year-old father's diet, especially his sugar intake. "The doctor says he has to watch his sugar or risk getting diabetes. He refuses to do so. When I go over to check on him, I throw out anything with sugar in it except fruit. He gets so angry at me but I know it's for his own good. Are you saying that's wrong?" she asked during a talk one evening. I responded, "Is your father mentally impaired in some way?"

"No, he's sharp as a tack. His memory is better than mine. It's just that he doesn't take care of himself the way he should."

"How he does or does not take care of himself is his business. How much or how little sugar he eats, is his own business. I know that's hard for you to hear because you love him so much and you want the best for him."

She shook her head, indicating she wasn't agreeing, and then I added, "How you feel about it is your business. You have every right in the world to say something like, 'Dad, when I look around the house and see all the cookies, pies, and cakes, I get scared, angry, and sad. I want the best health for you because I love you so much and so do your grandchildren.'"

She smiled. "That sounds better to me. I always hated having to speak to him the way I did. He would say, 'You are treating me like a child.' I just didn't know what else to say until now."

Likewise, parents have a difficult time detaching from the thoughts, feelings, and behaviors of their adult children. As parents, we are supposed to be connected with and feel our small children's feelings. That's right and natural. However, by the time their children enter adolescence, parents should almost completely separate their emotions from their children's, or those children may resort to destructive measures to demonstrate that they are separate.

Suzanne is one of the most spiritually and psychologically aware women that I've had the pleasure of knowing and working with. But she refuses to believe that her college-age daughter's business is not her business also. She has raised one of the most intelligent and mature daughters and yet she monitors her as if her daughter were nine instead of nineteen. Recently, she discovered that her daughter drank at parties and social events. She went through the young woman's purse when she came home for a visit and confiscated her driver's license. "If you are going to defy my rules about drinking until you are twenty-one, I will keep it until then. She told me, 'Drinking and driving is my business and you can't tell me otherwise,'" she said emphatically.

"So how is that going?" I asked.

"Well, I'm sure she's drinking anyway and she got a ticket last month for driving without a license. Her brother told me this because she hasn't spoken to me since I rifled through her purse and disregarded her privacy."

Another mother of a teen raised her hand after she spoke, "So what would compassionate assertive look like in this situation? I know my son drinks. He's twenty. I am on his case all the time about it and the angrier I get, the further apart we get."

"Say, 'I am angry, scared, disappointed, and do not want you to drink. I love you no matter what you do or don't do. I really, really am against drinking until it is legal and even then I'd rather not ever see you drink.' In other words, tell them what you feel, need, want, would like, and not like because that is your business." They both looked at me as if I were speaking a foreign language.

Mary Beth e-mailed me six months later and said, "I worked on this detachment thing with my son. I told him from my heart how I felt, not what he should or shouldn't do about the whole drinking thing. When I finished, he hugged me and he thanked me for being so respectful of him and his ability to make choices. Then he said, 'I'm going to choose not to drink for now. I love you, Mom.' He hasn't had a drink for five months. I don't worry about it at all."

Brody is a loving brother to his sister, Becky, and wants only the best for her. "I found out that her husband is cheating on her and I'm so angry I don't know what to do. Do I tell her or let her find out for herself? I don't know what is crossing the line here?" he said during a phone session.

"You said you're angry. Correct?"

"Very angry!"

"Have you thought about going to your brother-in-law and telling him how angry you are?" I asked.

"No. I haven't."

"Your feelings are your business. Your sister's marriage, good or bad, is not unless she comes to you and asks for information, guidance, input, or whatever she needs."

"She is an intelligent, grown woman," he replied.

"Right. Being compassionately assertive respects all that."

Because so many of us know so little about detaching with love and compassion, we often end up disconnecting or distancing ourselves with anger or rage from those overly involved in our emotional, financial, physical, sexual, or spiritual life. Disconnecting or distancing is usually done so out of regression. There is little or no compassion displayed by these actions and behaviors. We disconnect from those who don't know where they begin and end and where we begin and end. So the person who disconnects feels angry and the person who is being distanced from gets angry, enraged, hurt, and confused. There's nothing compassionate about that.

Detaching with love, I personally believe, is always the best option, but detaching with anger is sometimes necessary in certain situations. Distancing and disconnecting with rage is the least advisable and acceptable way to secure boundaries and stay in integrity with oneself. No one wins.

Compassionate assertiveness is always a win-win in the long run because it is born out of respect and appreciation for everyone concerned. When aggressive or passive/aggressive disconnect is initiated, there is usually some degree of not only anger but anxiety as well. This is why so many men and women say things like, "I don't want to tell Mom, Dad, my boss, or whoever how I feel because it might upset, hurt, destroy, or even kill that person, so I put up with all the undesirable behavior and tolerate the discomfort or even abuse," or things to that affect.

Not telling people what you feel because of how they might feel, think, or behave is grounded in anxiety that we will be abandoned, left, fired, divorced, or simply cut out of the will, and this produces huge amounts of anger and rage. Expressing your feelings in a compassionate way has no power over anyone except to the degree people let it have power over them. Telling your mother you don't like her cooking won't kill her. She's stronger than your dislike of her cooking, but refusing to go home and join her for a meal will cut her to the bone and has no compassion. Saying you don't like meatloaf is about you, not about her.

"I" Statements

This is where the "I" statements and looking a person in the eye comes in. Passive and passive/aggressive people will tell you more about *you* than they will about themselves. They'll tell you what you should do, feel, or say. When they finish trying to control you, they often think what they've communicated is "for your own good" or because they love and care about you.

Compassionately assertive people use the word *I* to tell you about themselves. The use of the word *you* in many conversational or confrontational situations is one of the most simultaneously passive and aggressive ways of speaking, because it is usually rooted in unsolicited criticism or advice giving. As you learned in chapter 2, when it comes to language, healthy anger is about "me" and destructive anger is about "you."

Criticism is a wild animal that is hard to tame. We've been taught and reminded that accepting criticism is just a necessary part of life. But unsolicited criticism is often a subtle act of rage by those who have received too much criticism in their past. If one has trouble saying no in general, it will be very difficult to say it to someone who thinks you or your work, thoughts, feelings, or speech needs to be judged.

Now, don't get me wrong—solicited and purposeful criticism positively changes people for the better. Take this very book you hold in your hands. I've asked my wife, who is a writer, to read it and give her critical assessment and feedback. I've asked another writer friend, Bill Stott, to read and give me feedback, and my editor has read and reread it and offered tons of advice and good suggestions regarding what to leave in and what to leave out. However, after this book is in print, I won't be open to criticism unless I specifically ask for it. But I sure will request and take lots more on the next one.

A boss or manager has to give criticism to his or her employees. Below are three different ways to do that.

Aggressive: "You got this wrong again. How many times have I got to show you? I don't think you'll ever get it."

Passive: "I'm sending this e-mail that terminates your employment. I should have said something to you a long time ago."

Compassionate Assertiveness: "Jim, I want to see you in my office tomorrow morning at 9:00 a.m. We're going to go over your strengths and weaknesses regarding your performance during your employee evaluation."

Passive, passive/aggressive, and even aggressive people fear confrontations and conflicts. Deep inside, they are anxious about the negative results their dysfunctional style always creates in everyone concerned, and as a result puts off facing problems for as long as possible, prolonging everyone's discomfort.

Compassionately assertive people who are able to recognize when they are or are not regressing or raging can expect much more satisfying outcomes, therefore they are less anxious. Should they find themselves with disproportionate feelings, they can take out paper and pen and take the Detour.

Confrontations will usually end in a win-win scenario with compassionately assertive people because the person they are interacting with will not have to leave the neocortex and head for the reptilian brain to fend off inappropriate, raging words and actions. They also know how to say no if necessary; they can stand up for themselves, assert their rights and feelings, create and defend boundaries, and set reasonable limits. Compassionate assertive men and women have no intent to hurt or damage and can refrain from overreacting. They can wait for the best time and place and do not dump their past history onto the present person nor erase them with the present-person/people eraser— regression and rage.

Compassionately assertive people know they don't have to explain or justify their feelings, thoughts, or actions to anyone unless they want or need to.

Matthew, a young, stocky college senior, asked, "If I tell my girlfriend that I don't want to meet her parents, don't I have to tell her why?" during *The Anger Solution* seminar. "No, you don't have to," I said. "You can choose to if that's what you want, but adults don't have to tell another adult what is going on inside them."

"I'm just not ready to meet them. I don't feel we've known each other long enough but I don't want to disappoint her or give her the wrong idea."

"Her disappointments or ideas are her business and being authentic and true is your business."

"It sounds a little selfish to me, but I know every time I don't listen to that little voice inside me that knows what I need to do and don't, it always comes out pretty badly."

In dysfunctional families, many people have been told not to share feelings or emotions, or have only been permitted in some cases if the person experiencing them could explain them adequately and satisfactory enough to those who might be listening.

Matthew explored this truth about his family. "If me or my sister cried, Dad would say things like, 'Tell me why you're crying,' and it was always never a good enough reason for him no matter what we said. He'd say something like, 'That's no reason for a big kid like you to be a cry baby.' I guess I've always felt I had to explain any feeling I've ever had. I guess you're saying it's now a choice. That feels a lot better."

Not only do compassionately assertive people not have to explain their feelings, they don't have to ask permission to discuss them when they're ready or listen to others tell theirs if they are not willing or able to hear it.

Passive: "If it's all right with you, I'd like to tell you how I really feel about _____."

Aggressive: "Sit down, we're going to talk about _____ whether you want to or not."

Compassionately Assertive: "I need to tell you how I feel about _____. I would like us to sit down and talk about this."

Passive people ask permission unnecessarily, under the guise of being polite and well mannered, telegraphing a presumption that the other person will not comply with their request.

Passive: "I'm wondering if you wouldn't mind doing the shopping today."

Compassionate Assertive: "I'm not able to go grocery shopping. I'd like for you to go today."

Passive: "I know this might not work for you, but could we come to your house for dinner if it's not too much to ask?"

Compassionate Assertive: "I would like to come to your house for dinner; I'm too tired to cook."

Passive and aggressive people don't respect themselves, usually due to low self-esteem and low self-worth. Because truly compassionately assertive people respect themselves, they extend that respect and civility to others. As Judith McClure says in her book *Assertiveness for Women*, "Civility is ethical behavior towards others. Assertiveness is ethical behavior towards ourselves." We can't show the former if we don't embody the latter.

Passive and aggressive people play out their rage by stereotyping, racial profiling, sexism, homophobia, and other disrespectful and damaging ways of behaving and thinking. Compassionately assertive people can argue, disagree, and disengage, but they are aware that disrespecting and denigrating are not adult behaviors. If they must judge or even engage in criticism, the focus is on the *behavior*, not the person or a group.

Bill stood up during a seminar and said that he disliked "all Jewish people." When I asked him if he would take a sheet of paper and take the Detour, he agreed. Later that day, after the lunch break, he came up to me and said, "During lunch, I answered those questions and I remembered something I hadn't thought of in over three decades. My father had a small business in New York. The building was owned by a Jewish man and without any notice, or at least that's the way I remember it, he sold the building and told my dad to get out. I don't think I've ever had any bad dealings or interactions with Jewish people in my adult life."

When compassionately assertive people do regress, rage, stereotype, or judge a person instead of that person's behavior, they apologize as soon as they recognize their remarks and behaviors were inappropriate. Passive and aggressive people are more prone to rationalize or deny their rudeness, rash, or dysfunctional language or conduct. If they do try to take some responsibility, it is more often accompanied by the words "I'm sorry" and then they proceed to tell you why they really shouldn't apologize or that the person who was disrespected don't really deserve an apology.

"Jason is always saying he's sorry about this and that," said Clarice in a phone consultation. "But I never feel like he really means it. It's like they are just the right words at the moment. I'm tired of it. I want an apology and I want it to be sincere. Last night was our twenty-fifth wedding anniversary and we were supposed to meet our best friends at our favorite restaurant. He was an hour and a half late. As soon as he sat down out came his usual, 'I'm sorry,' and then he went on to say, 'I got this call from a very high-dollar client and the guy just kept talking and talking and wouldn't shut up. I kept trying to bring the conversation to a close but he just wouldn't stop.' I got up and said, 'Then maybe you should have had dinner with him, he's so damn important,' and I left the restaurant and went outside and threw my purse against the wall."

Compassionately assertive people might say something like: "I apologize for being late. I hope you'll forgive me and I'll do my very best to make sure this doesn't happen again." It is an active, responsible, and accountable statement of error and a commitment to change their behavior as a way to make amends for the hurt or wrong they have done.

The Compassionate Assertive Constitution

In the nineteenth and early twentieth century, a term was applied to men and women to denote strength in character and personality. It would be said of such people that they had a "strong constitution" because they could handle themselves physically, emotionally, mentally, and spiritually in difficult circumstances and situations. A weak constitution meant just the opposite—that they were fearful, lacked circumspection, and would probably collapse under adversity.

Another term used more commonly in the 1940s and even today, thanks in part to the gifted writer Ernest Hemingway, is "grace under pressure." As you can see by now, regressed people, no matter what style of rage they practice, perpetuate, and perpetrate, is anything but indicative of a "strong constitution" or "grace under pressure." The compassionately assertive person is the embodiment of both terms.

The following compassionate assertive constitution is an example of one person's commitment to maintaining grace under pressure in both personal and professional situations:

- I will stand up and speak out my feelings, wants, needs, and desires.
- I will speak directly to anyone I am engaging with.
- I will stop participating in relationship triangles of any kind.
- I will establish strong boundaries and be emotionally, physically, and mentally prepared to defend them.
- I will set good, healthy limits and honor them.

- I will treat every person, regardless of the relationship, race, creed, or color, with the utmost respect and dignity.
- When I make a boundary error, mistake, or violation, I will apologize and change my behavior as soon as humanly possible.
- I am more interested in communicating clearly and cleanly than in winning at all costs.
- I will pay attention to those who are speaking, looking them in the eye whenever possible.
- I will practice using "I" statements to express myself whenever possible, telling others about me instead of about them.
- When I find or catch myself regressing, raging, or slipping back into my past history, I will take all necessary steps to return to the present moment/situation or person as soon as possible.
- I will develop and participate in relationships that are healthy, functional, open and honest, nonshaming and nonjudgmental, and whose participants offer helpful criticism only when requested.
- I will increase daily my ability to empathize with fellow adults.
- I will be a better person in direct proportion to the degree I release my anger appropriately, which gives me and everyone safety, security, and trust.
- I will not explain or justify my feelings, emotions, behaviors, or thoughts to anyone unless I choose to do so.

- I will always try to reduce stress, exhaustion, hunger, and illness so I can live healthier, regress less, and be vulnerable and available to the people I care about.
- I will focus on a person's *behavior* and not the person with whom I may be in conflict or disagree.
- I will correct passive speaking by not relying on clichés or worn, tired phrases, but by being creative and inventive yet to the point.
- I will compliment and give credit for others' accomplishments and achievements.
- I will welcome and gladly receive compliments and credit for my own.
- I will care for others but never undermine their integrity or care or take them as if they are not clear-thinking, mature adults.

Completing the Four Compassionate Assertive Statements

These four statements, if considered, contemplated, and completed, will decrease anger, eliminate rage, enhance clarity and communication, diminish misunderstanding, and work for virtually every issue, conflict, decision, and interaction, whether it be personal or professional. These four compassionate assertive statements are used by my clients and workshop participants over the years. Fill in the blanks as appropriate to your own situation.

1. This is what I want: _____.

2. This is what I need: _____.
3. This is what I *will not* do to get the above wants and needs met, achieved, or accomplished: _____.
4. This is what I *will* do to get these wants and needs met, achieved, or accomplished: _____.

Sandy's main problem in her marriage—as she identified it—was that her husband worked all the time. "He works as much as eighty hours a week. I know he wants a good life for me and the kids, but we hardly ever see him and when we do, he's exhausted or asleep."

"What do you want?" I asked her to write it down. Wants are your best-case scenarios, your fantasies fulfilled, your magic wand waved and presto-chango, you get them, no questions asked.

"I want more time for us and the kids and I want him to work less," she said after taking a few moments.

"What do you *need* regarding this problem or issue?" That is the second statement, but note this is considerably different and usually more difficult to answer. Needs are not nearly as negotiable as wants, and in some cases they are completely non-negotiable and not open for compromise as wants may be. Needs are more like food, air, water, sleep, or love; you have to have them, can't live without them, and they must be strongly asserted and stood up for, no matter what.

Sandy took about ten or fifteen minutes on this part. After she wrote she looked up and said, "I need one evening every week for just the two of us to talk, make love, or just cuddle and watch a movie. I need him to take better care of himself so he can be more present and available for our children," she paused. "That sounds so selfish. Am I being too self-centered to need this? Maybe I'm too demanding."

"Let's see," I said. "Tell me how you have gone about trying to get those needs and wants met in the past?"

"Well, that's easy," she said, laughing. "I just nagged, complained, and criticized him for the last couple of years. I guess that's being more selfish than saying straight out what I need."

"Okay, next, what will you *not* do to get these wants and needs met?"

"I won't nag or criticize him anymore. I won't try and be both mother and father to the kids to make up for his lack of interaction and attention. I won't speak badly about him anymore."

"What you won't do is more about setting good boundaries, establishing your limits, not raging and regressing, being codependent or passive, or a martyr. Okay, Sandy. Now what *will* you do to get your wants and needs met?"

Again, she took about ten or fifteen minutes before answering.

"I will speak my truth. I will set good boundaries and limits. I will support him in any way I can, even if that means my going back to work at least part-time. I will watch household expenses and my spending so he won't feel so pressured by money issues. I will love him, no matter what. I will tell him so and how much I appreciate all the things he does for this family." She took a deep breath and let out a heavy sigh. "Why weren't we taught to talk like this before?"

Then she asked when the best time was to do this exercise. The absolute best time is when you and the other person are not regressed. When you're rested and refreshed and have not argued or fought recently about a particular issue. Sadly, most people try to tell other people their wants and needs right in the middle or at the end of a major confrontation, when everyone is regressed, exhausted, or scared, and no one gets heard. Or everyone hears the other person's wants and needs as more pressure, stress, ultimatums, or threats.

When I state this, so many will say that when things are going smoothly, it seems unfair to bring up those ugly issues. What is really unfair and more hurtful and damaging is holding in these things until they erupt and get blurted out with no regard for the rage that usually follows.

Here's another example using the Four Compassionate Assertive Statements: Mark works at a building supply company for a boss who is less than appreciative of his effort. "I've worked there for three and a half years and the man has never once complimented me or given me a raise, and he has me managing a section of the store I know the least about. I keep asking to be transferred into the yard and garden section. I know plants and flowers better than anyone at the store. I stay frustrated and angry most of my working hours," he said, looking as disgusted as he felt with the whole situation.

"Okay, got it. What do you want?"

"I want to be in the garden section. I want my boss to appreciate how hard I work and to tell me so ever blue moon or so. I want a raise in pay and I want to enjoy where I work. Yeah, that's about it."

"What do you need?" He answered as quickly as anyone I've worked with.

"I need respect, appreciation, and to enjoy where I work. That's not asking too much, is it?"

"What will you not do to get your wants and needs met in this situation?"

On this one he took some time and then said, "I'm not sure." He paused and thought. "I will not work anywhere or for anyone that doesn't appreciate me. My boss needs to eventually place me where I can be the best at what I do."

"What will you do to get what your wants and needs met?" He took some time and wrote this in his journal and then said, "I will ask my boss for a performance evaluation at least every six months and I will tell him I am not being used efficiently in the department I'm in and request a transfer into the garden department as soon as that is possible."

"How does that feel to say all of this with such clarity and consciousness?" I asked.

"Great! And you know, my boss is a pretty smart fellow or he wouldn't be in the position he is in, so I bet he'll listen to me and then if he doesn't respond within, say, three to six months at the most, then I'll look for a place where my strengths can be put to good use. I guess you'd call that *setting a limit*, right?"

"Right. Good work and good luck!"

You can see in both examples that Sandy and Mark are both going for a win-win and if their respective counterparts can hear them—and they probably will, given how appropriate Sandy and Mark's respective side of the discussion will be—there will be much more satisfying outcomes. Because they will not rage, regress, shame, blame, criticize, or judge, they are being compassionate first towards themselves and then in extending compassion to the others in their lives. Sandy's children will benefit, Mark's family will benefit, because being compassionately assertive whenever possible comes with incalculable fringe and essential benefits.

The 5+5+5 Exercise for Increasing Clarity and Compassionate Assertiveness

Sometimes, especially when regressed, we say five thousand words trying to convey our feelings, wants, and needs. Then the person hearing them looks at us and scratches his or her head and says something like, "So what exactly are you trying to say?" With an exhausted or exasperated tone in our voice we begin another five thousand with the hope that the other person will get what it is we're still not saying.

I developed this exercise several years ago from actively listening to clients and workshop participants as they tried to explain their issues, pain, feelings, or concerns. Nine out of ten would say, usually within the first five minutes, exactly what was bothering them . . . and then continue on for thirty or more minutes. When I see this happening, I will often pull out this exercise, and now you can do the same at home or at work.

Here is how to do the 5+5+5 exercise on your own:

1. Write in five minutes what you are angry, regressed, or enraged about. Note: Don't actively time yourself, but try to keep a notion of 5 minutes.

2. When you finish, take note of how long you took (note sometimes it is six, seven, or even as much as ten minutes). Now, write the same thing using only five sentences.

3. Now, write it in five words.

Beverly is a great example of this experience in adult-to-adult communication. It is especially great for adult-to-child communication because children's vocabulary and attention span is usually much shorter.

"Tell me what is triggering your regression and silent rage," I said.

She immediately began, "My teenage daughter is cutting me out of her life. We used to be such good friends. Now she doesn't say two words to me a week. It's like we're strangers. It all started when she turned eleven . . . "

And so she went for almost ten more minutes, and when she paused, I suggested we do the 5+5+5 exercise. She immediately agreed.

"Now tell me in five sentences how you are feeling and thinking about this whole thing between you and your daughter."

She began talking and went a few sentences over five. "Now tell me in five words or less," I said.

She started crying. "I miss her and I'm angry and scared. That was more than five, wasn't it," she said, wiping away the tears.

"Have you ever said those exact words to her?" I asked gently.

"No, I do what you say not to do at your *Anger Solution* workshops. I tend to preach, teach, criticize, and all that other stuff, and really I just want her to know that I love her and miss her. God, it's so hard to be so direct, or at least I guess it is until you have some practice."

And practice is the key to mastering being compassionately assertive.

Chapter 8

Anger and Emotional Intelligence

E motional intelligence is a relatively new field of study popularized by Daniel Goleman's book *Emotional Intelligence* that came out in 1995. For many years we have been focused on IQ and how to test it, increase it, debate it, and celebrate it. The phrase, "He or she is a genius!" is praise equal to he or she is president or pope.

The funny thing about IQ is that it is relatively fixed by a person's twentieth birthday. It may go up or down by a point or two during the rest of one's lifetime, but for the most part, it is set in early adulthood.

However, EQ, our emotional intelligence quotient, can be increased every day for the rest of our life. We can learn to increase our range of emotions, express our emotions clearly, and use this kind of intelligence where and when the intellect alone fails. This interest in people's ability to have a greater connection to their own emotional life is being seen by some as being possibly more important than one's IQ.

In today's business centers, emotional intelligence is becoming a huge factor in employment practices. Twenty-five years ago, a person with an MBA from Harvard was guaranteed a top position in many firms, right out of college. If this person was top of the class, he or she climbed to the top of the corporate ladder. Things are changing. A B-average student with an MBA from the local university who demonstrates a superior ability to know his or her feelings and emotions is more likely to be prized by potential employers, compared with a brilliant student who lacks basic social skills. Many companies are aware that a person with a greater ability to listen and empathize will know how to manage others and relate to customers or client needs. As Goleman says, "Empathy builds on self-awareness: the more open we are to our own emotions, the more skilled we will be in reading feelings."

You may recall empathy is one of the keys to bringing people out of regression and the often accompanying rage. Think how valuable a customer service manager would be, who has a greater ability to empathize when dealing with an irate customer.

Exploring our angry feelings is a door we walk through to increase our emotional intelligence and make us more conscious, attuned to our own motivations, prejudices, and judgments.

Where does anger fit in with emotional intelligence? The father and mother who have highly developed emotional lives and are more in touch with their feelings will not shame, blame, ridicule, and rage at their children. Emotionally intelligent parents regress less and catch their regressions sooner, and they do much less emotional damage not only to their children but to each other.

Emotionally intelligent politicians who know the difference between anger and rage are in better control of their own behavior in critical situations. Presidents who have the greater abilities to empathize with people in particular and other countries in general will be more diplomatic, and so on.

Emotional and thus physical violence diminishes and all but disappears in direct proportion to the development of our emotional intelligence as an individual, a family, a community, or a country. People will still have differing opinions and will still argue, and yes, people with a higher IQ may have a better debating ability and a greater vocabulary, but people with a greater EQ will know and feel their positions strongly but will not believe they have to defend them at all costs because, at the end of an argument, win or lose, they walk away not only knowing who they are but that ultimately they'd rather be happy than right.

It is emotional intelligence that increases our ability to live a happier and more authentic life. Since anger is one of the most basic emotions, if we can't feel it in the moment it occurs and express it appropriately to the approximate person, it is difficult to be truly authentic in all our relationships.

Part of living an authentic life is being who we are and feeling what we feel in the present moment. To some degree, most of us are land-locked in our past and tend to perform the roles we were given in the tragic-comedy of our childhoods. Some play the hero who will save the family. Others play the part of the victim for their whole life. Peacemaker, lost child, star athlete, loser, or clown: All are roles that are hard to shake.

Where there are roles, there is a rage. If people feel they have to continue playing the part of the dutiful son or daughter or the perfect parent or partner, there is little room for connection or even conversation outside the parameter of that role. Stanley, who is now in his midseventies, said during a session with his forty-year-old son, "I am tired of being a parent. I want and need you to see me as a man." Randy, who is fifty-eight, said to me over the phone, "No matter how much I achieve, how much money I make, I keep looking for my father's approval. He walks into my office and I become the same boy that screwed up at nineteen and he plays the disapproving dad."

When roles clash, rage ensues. You don't really relate to me, you relate to the role I play, and vice versa.

A couple of really nice parents came to see me about their "kid" who is having a great deal of trouble with alcohol, drugs, and the legal system. I asked them how old the "kid" was. "He'll be thirty-six his next birthday. We just want to know how we can be better parents to him. We've tried everything. We've put him through half a dozen rehabs and treatment facilities."

"Have you considered trying to stop playing the role of *being good parents* to a man who you still place in the role of designated problem child?" Perhaps it is time to drop the parent role and just be people who must have lots of anger and fear, given what you've said, and communicate it appropriately to this person you care so much and deeply for?"

"We never thought of that," said the man to his wife. "Exactly how does one go about doing that after seeing ourselves as parents for more than thirty years?"

"Good question. Let's begin by doing some anger work."

Final Thoughts

In over two decades of facilitating, training, and conducting workshops and seminars on anger, rage, regression, and TDM, I have found that sadness, sorrow, fear, and hurt will almost always accompany anger and rage. If you decide to use the tools, information, and exercises to catch yourself before going into regression and therefore remove the rage from your life so that you can express your anger appropriately, come out of passive behaviors, and set good boundaries and limits, then I'm pretty certain you will be open to the following suggestion. Take the Detour and explore, experience, and express the grief that is inherent in most adults' lives.

Anger is for getting out of stuck places and grief work is for having been stuck for so long. Grief work acknowledges the loss of time, love, relationships, jobs, or anything that has hurt your heart.

Let's say in the past your body has contained a thousand pounds of unexpressed anger and rage. Your same body has held back a thousand or more tears. Those tears sometimes come out while watching a sad movie or reading about a tragedy. And that is to be celebrated. However, real grieving is about acknowledging the sad parts of your own life and mourning the small and large tragedies that everyone has their fair share of.

I knew this young college professor who tells the story of how his first love in college left him. "I was devastated beyond description and belief. When she left, I started crying and I thought I'd never stop. I cried every day. This was most extraordinary because I couldn't remember the last time I cried. We were taught that big boys don't cry and there I was sobbing into my cereal in the mornings and crying myself to sleep for several months. I finally went to see my ex-girlfriend and begged her to come back and told her that I'd do anything she asked. She said something that hit me so hard I'll never forget it. 'Your sorrow and sadness is too deep, too intense, too much to be just about losing me. I feel you have touched the sorrow that has been in you for a long time and if I were to come back now, you'd stop and you'd never let out all the pain that I've always known you've held in. I love you too much to do that.' She was right. I'll always be deeply grateful to her for that." That young man was me twenty-five years ago and wrote about it in my first book, *The Flying Boy: Healing the Wounded Man*.

Unexpressed grief and sadness can be just as quickly triggered as anger and rage. By using The Detour Method and other exercises in this book you can, when you're ready, let it out and you will find this, too, will allow you to be more fully in the present moment, regress less, and be even more compassionately assertive because you'll be a lot less afraid of "losing" and less inclined to "win" at all costs. You will be a more compassionate, empathetic, attention giving, and receiving person who acts, talks, thinks, behaves, and interacts with others as a mature adult, loving partner, parent, friend, boss, employee, son or daughter. I believe this is why you picked this book up in the first place.

Both anger and grief work can be done by yourself. You can pay attention to your feelings, give yourself time to experience those pent-up emotions, contact a part of yourself that has been in hiding, and express and release any and all feelings from childhood up to this very moment.

Like I said in the previous section, titled *"Whom to Take the Detour With,"* I suggest and encourage you not to be scared to find safe people you can trust, to let out some of your sadness with. This is especially true if you tend to isolate yourself and withdraw from people.

When you do get to your long-buried emotions with others, you are working simultaneously on your feelings of being embarrassed while releasing emotions. You will work on increasing your sense of self-worth by accepting the attention, empathy, and time from others. You will reduce your private shame for having such strong emotions and others will benefit not only by experiencing their own anger and grief vicariously but by having a sense of fulfillment and joy for helping you release yours in the process. Everybody wins.

For over twenty years I have suggested creating a network or community of safe people such as those who attend, participate, and practice emotional release work with the support of P.E.E.R.s (see "Primary, Emotional, Energy, Recovery") or therapists, sponsors, mentors, and guides.

You've heard the old joke: "How do you get to Carnegie Hall?" "Practice, practice, practice." How do you become someone who is in touch with his or her emotions, emotionally intelligent, emotionally present and available, vulnerable yet safe, trusting and trustworthy? Practice, practice, practice The Detour Method.

How to Contact the Author

For more information on John Lee's *Anger Solution* workshops and schedules or for further information on books, audio, corporate presentations, and private consultations, please visit John Lee's Web site at www.johnleebooks.com or contact him at:

John Lee
John Lee Books and Seminars
553 County Road 624
Mentone, AL 35984
Tel: 678-494-1296

ACKNOWLEDGMENTS

My gratitude goes to a person in Austin, Texas, who showed me just how much I needed to work on my own anger issues, never suspecting that I would write, teach, and coach to thousands over the last twenty-plus years.

My wife, Susan Lee, who helped me with this and other books in so many ways that I can't list them all nor thank her adequately. Her talent runs through this book like a gentle river.

My agent, Penny Nelson, at Manus Literary Agency for her support, patience, and belief in me and my work—no percentage could ever repay you for how much I'm in your debt.

My editor at Da Capo, Renee Sedliar, is one in a million. Her "old school" way of working with a writer and his words was a huge blessing. She transformed a project into a process and then into a product that I hope will help enhance and encourage the lives of many people so they'll be freer to engage their emotions and expand their range of feelings, allowing them to connect, communicate, and cooperate.

A special thanks to my assistant, Beth Easler, for her typing and re-typing and typing again.

And most of all I thank the people who have supported me and been there for me all these many years—Bill Stott, Robert Bly, Dan

Jones, Karen Blicher, Vijay Director, Connie Burns, Tim Schaller, Kathy McClelland, and all the people in P.E.E.R. A special thanks to those who have been my clients and workshop participants. I also want to thank you, the reader, for picking up this book and having the courage, caring, and commitment to work on yourself and letting me have the privilege and honor to be a small part of your healing journey.

Further Suggested Reading

Damasio, Antonio. *The Feeling of What Happens*. Boston: Harcourt, Inc., 1999.

Goleman, Daniel. *Emotional Intelligence*. New York: Bantam, 1995.

Jones, Dan. *P.E.E.R. Teaching Stories*. San Rafael, CA: Mandala Publishing, 2001.

Lee, John. *Facing the Fire: Experiencing and Expressing Anger Appropriately*. New York: Bantam, 1993.

———. *Growing Yourself Back Up: Understanding Emotional Regression*. New York: Three Rivers Press, 2001.

———. *The Missing Peace: Solving the Anger Problem for Alcoholics/Addicts and Those Who Love Them*. Deerfield Beach, FL: HCI, 2006.

Levine, Peter. *Waking the Tiger*. Berkeley, CA: North Atlantic Books, 1997.

Pert, Candace. *Molecules of Emotion*. New York: Scribner, 1997.

Richo, David. *How to Be in Adult Relationships*. Boston: Shambhala Publications, 2002.

Wood, Peter. *A Bee in the Mouth: Anger in America Now*. New York: Encounter Books, 2006.

INDEX